HOMOSEXUALITY:
A BIBLICAL WORLDVIEW

ROGER L. PRICE SR. , MAHS, MAPC

TRILOGY

Trilogy Christian Publishers

A Wholly Owned Subsidiary of Trinity Broadcasting Network

2442 Michelle Drive

Tustin, CA 92780

For information, address Trilogy Christian Publishing

Rights Department, 2442 Michelle Drive, Tustin, CA 92780.

Trilogy Christian Publishing/ TBN and colophon are trademarks of Trinity Broadcasting Network.

For information about special discounts for bulk purchases, please contact Trilogy Christian Publishing.

Trilogy Disclaimer: The views and content expressed in this book are those of the author and may not necessarily reflect the views and doctrine of Trilogy Christian Publishing or the Trinity Broadcasting Network.

10 9 8 7 6 5 4 3 2 1

Library of Congress Cataloging-in-Publication Data is available.

ISBN 979-9-89041-708-4

ISBN (ebook) 979-9-89041-709-1

CONTENTS

INTRODUCTION

To address the issue of homosexuality, the current direction of our culture, and the narrative regarding several hot button issues, it is important to consider a few different concepts. The three major concepts I want you as a reader to consider are truth, perception, and worldview. In particular, the worldview that is most significant is, and the focus of this book is, a biblical worldview. Today people are pressed to decide if there is such a thing as truth and if so, what is truth and where can I find truth? What about the things that I was taught as a child, things that not only I and my family have been taught for generations going back as far as any knowledge of our existence? I am referring to such things that date back to the beginning of the existence of humanity as we know it. I speak of a time when it was easy to see and to agree with certain facts such as two plus two equals four. Things such as pronouncing, "It's a boy" or "It's a girl" upon first glance at the biological components that were observed and examined. I speak of a time when it was understood by reasonable men and women that there is a difference between people's objective conclusions and subjective conclusions. It was understood that the objective things provided the best opportunity to see and understand things as they really were, while the subjective opinions and conclusions would more likely be influenced by our personal experiences and biases. There were fact and reality-based universal truths that were consistent and accompanied by predictable outcomes which we could all rely on, live our lives by, and raise our children and grandchildren on.

Then the world is introduced to "postmodernism" that, in large part tell us that virtually everything that we have believed in the past was wrong. All our philosophers, physicians, engineers, mathematicians, scientists, historians, and our theologians who don't agree with these current claims of the LGBTQ and Transgender proponents were all wrong regarding their conclusions about truth, facts, and reality. According to the postmodernist, they "...argue that what we call reality is not an exact replica of what is out there, but rather socially or communally constructed through language. One cannot hope to finally discover an elusive truth:" (Goldenberg & Goldenberg, 2013, p. 369). What you will find is that, while there are many social and communal constructs, truth is, categorically, not and cannot be socially or communally constructed by any means. Contrary to the postmodernist that posits "truth is elusive", truth can be discovered. Truth, in fact, is and can only be revealed and discovered and never constructed.

I affirm that while I recognize that all truth is God's truth, I further affirm that the Judeo- Christian Bible, in particular, as used in this book, contains the most consistent, most comprehensive, most accurate and by far the most important body of truths that can, and ever will be revealed or discovered. Therefore, all the conclusions I make in this book are intended to be based on a biblical worldview. I encourage each of you who read this book to do your own search of the scriptures regarding the issue of homosexuality and see whether the conclusions drawn in this book is in fact consistent with the teachings of the said Bible(s).

Please also know that having a biblical worldview doesn't mean accepting and believing the things in the Bible that you like and rejecting that portion of the Bible that teaches things that you don't like or agree with. For example, Jesus rebuked the Pharisees and Scribes for doing just that when He said to them, "You study the Scriptures diligently because you think that in them you have eternal life. These are the very Scriptures that testify about me." (John 5:39 NIV) Here Jesus is saying that the same scriptures which cause you to believe that you have eternal life are the same scriptures that tell people about Him. Jesus was saying to the Pharisees that they accept as true what the Bible says about them having eternal life, but they reject portions of the same scriptures that testify about Him. Oftentimes those who talk about the importance of love, tolerance, and acceptance based on the scriptures, reject other scriptures that clearly list behaviors that are inappropriate, unacceptable, or just plain wrong and sinful. It is my prayer that this book will be instrumental in helping you, your family, relatives, friends, and acquaintances to know the truth about homosexuality and remain committed to standing firm on the truth of scripture and conducting your lives accordingly.

Finally, per the admonition of the Apostle Paul and John who respectively stated, "Consider what I say; and the Lord give thee understanding in all things." (2 Timothy 2:7, KJV) "Then you will know the truth, and the truth will set you free." (John 8:32, NIV)

THE TRUTH

According to Aristotle, "To say what is that is not, or of what is not that it is, is false, while to say of what is that it is, and of what is not that it is not, is true." Retrieved from https://www.azquotes.com/quote/766608.

Now that seems quite logical and reasonable. This statement is made by a person who is considered to be one of the greatest critical thinkers of all times and the top three most famous Greek philosophers. Not only was Aristotle a philosopher, but he was also a teacher, logician, and scientist. Aristotle provides anyone who will hear and receive it a simple and straightforward definition of the truth which those in our current world just can't seem to get, or just simply refuse to accept and that is, "...to say of what is that it is, and of what is not that it is not, is true."

Perhaps the reason it was so easy for Aristotle to understand and articulate truth is that his concept of truth was not impacted by his political agenda. Today, the idea of such things as truth and facts are now influenced and determined by people's political and personal agendas. People are changing that which is truth and consistent with facts to fit their political narrative and personal preferences. Truth does not have such flexibility. A Hindu proverb states, "Denying the truth doesn't change the facts." (Author Unknown)

Arthur Schopenhauer tells us, "All truth passes through three states. First, it is ridiculed. Second, it is violently opposed. Third, it is accepted as being self-evident." That indeed appears to be the process of truth, at least it used to be. Today, like never before, truth is violently opposed and under no circumstance are certain people willing to accept the truth, even when it is "self-evident."

Pilate, during the last trial of Jesus, when he appeared to be seeking a way to let Jesus go, asked the question, "What is truth?" (John 18:38 KJV) A technical definition of truth suggests that truth is the reality, fact, and certainty of a thing. It is veracity, verity, veridicality, authenticity, genuineness, and that which is without deception, free of pretense, void of falsity, without equivocation, evasion, and hedging. Aristotle also stated, "Falsehood is mean and culpable, and truth is noble and worthy of praise." Retrieved from https://www/thoughtco.com/aristotle-quotes-117130

People who are honest and truthful will tell you the truth, but those who are dishonest and deceitful will lie to you, according to a biblical proverb that states, "An honest witness tells the truth; a false witness tells lies." (Proverbs 12:17, NIV) It is truly neither right nor fair to judge people by anything other than their character. Nor is it healthy or wise to do so. The Bible tells us that the truth should be obtained and never parted with, not for any price. "Get the truth, and never sell it..." (Proverbs 23:23, NLT)

A very important thing to know about truth is that truth is inherently protective. Truth is a prophylactic. I like the definition given by Dr. William C. Shiel Jr. in his definition of prophylactic according rxlist.com/prophylactic. He says that a prophylactic is "A preventive measure. The word comes from the Greek for 'an advance guard.' This is an apt term for a measure taken to fend off a disease or another unwanted consequence." Retrieved from https://www.rxlist.com/prophylactic/definition.htm

It is somewhat ironic that a significant number of people in our world today who purport to care about us and whose actions are designed to help us and protect us, are, the very ones who will cancel all who disagree with them are the biggest deceivers and liars. Then they engage in cover ups. They don't want others to know of the consequences or the outcomes that result from the lies that they told you.

Remember this, the devil and his human emissaries have an exclusive threefold goal, to kill, steal, and to destroy. It was Jesus that revealed to us the unequivocal goal of the devil. Jesus states, "The thief comes only to steal and kill and destroy; I have come that they may have life and have it to the full." (John 10:10

NIV) Here we see that the devil's goals are exclusive. While the NIV uses the word "only" for the actual Greek word, I think the Greek word is better translated as "not," as KJV translates it. So, what we see is, the devil doesn't come to you, regardless as to how or when he comes to you, with any purposes, goals or intents but to steal, kill, and to destroy.

Anyone, regardless of their race, gender, political affiliation, religious ideology, or position of authority, who will lie to you has an ulterior motive and an agenda that is not in your best interest and is ultimately of the devil. Consequently, their lies are ultimately of the devil and are irreversibly destructive and deadly.

Remember, it is extremely difficult, if not impossible, for evil to make inroads into our lives without the use of a lie or lies. Historically and biblically speaking, one of the devil's most powerful and effective tactics is to tell half-truths, or mix the truth with a lie. If you are totally uninformed, he can just tell you a complete lie. However, if you are somewhat informed, he will mix the truth with a lie, as in the case of Adam and Eve. For example, the devil, referred to here as the serpent, approaches Eve and, through his deceitfulness, deceives her. The Bible tells us, "Now the serpent was more subtle than any beast of the field which the LORD God had made. And he said unto the woman, Yea, hath God said, Ye shall not eat of every tree of the garden?" (Genesis 3:1, KJV) However, Eve knows the truth, as we will see in her response. The devil uses a sleight of hand by misquoting what God said. However, Eve corrects him as she responds by saying, "And the woman said unto the serpent, We may eat of the fruit of the trees of the garden: But of the fruit of the tree which *is* in the midst of the garden, God hath said, Ye shall not eat of it, neither shall ye touch it, lest ye die." (Genesis 3:1-3 KJV) Note, the devil said, "every" or "any" tree, which was a categorically false statement and totally opposite of what God had said. God gave them the liberty to eat of every single tree in the garden with the exception of one.

Again, never forget my earlier statement of the protective nature of truth and the biblical admonition regarding the truth, to never sell it. And remember that the devil had no power or influence over the woman or the world except through the woman and man believing and embracing a lie. Believing and acting on the lie that was told to them by the devil gave him an inroad into their lives, into the lives of the human race, into the world and the whole of creation that is irreversibly destructive and deadly. As truth is inherently healthy and life-giving, all lies are inherently harmful and destructive.

Even though there were immediate and notable consequences of their belief in the big lie, the ultimate consequence is yet to be experienced. So it is for all who will believe the lies that people are pushing regarding homosexuality. Though we see some immediate and notable negative consequences, the ultimate consequences, which are inevitable, will be irreversibly destructive and deadly, as biblical history has shown us. It was Ryan Bigge who said, "The truth hurts for a little while. A lie hurts forever." https://www.goodreads.com/author/show/130074.Ryan_Bigge

Finally, truth is more than just a concept. Truth is a substance. It was Jesus, who was the first and only person who embodied and personified truth by the way he lived and by stating, "I am the way, the truth, and the life." Truth emanates from the character, nature and makeup of God.

We have two very powerful divine truth and admonitions. First, there is the revelatory truth written by the Apostle Paul, "For we can do nothing against the truth, but for the truth." (2 Corinthians 13:8 KJV) Second, we have the admonition by James, "But if you have bitter envy and self-seeking in your hearts, do not boast and lie against the truth." (James 3:14 NKJV)

THE PERCEPTION DECEPTION

According to an article by Visweswaran Balasubramanian, What is Truth? A Philosophical Approach, the phrase "Perception Deception" is attributed to Aldous Huxley. According to Balasubramanian, Huxley who stated, "There are things known and there are things unknown, and in between are the doors of perception." He goes on to say, "Perception is a dynamic conflict between the attempts of an outer world to impose an actuality on us and our efforts to transform this into a self-centered perspective." His belief that in a world of relativism and perspectivism, "our perception is greatly hijacked through something he would call the "perception deception."

Huxley lists several contributing factors to the perception deception. The first is what he called, "Obscurantism, which is referred to as the practice of deliberately preventing the facts or full details of something from being known."

Second, Indoctrination, which he defines as "the process of teaching a person or group to accept a set of beliefs uncritically." Third, Selective Perception, which is "the process by which we perceive what we want to hear while ignoring opposing viewpoints." Retrieved from https://timesofindia.indiatimes.com/readersblog/mycosmos/what-is-truth-a-philosophical-approach-28803/.

These three major factors of the perception deception are on full display in our world today and is front and center in our cultural war. There is a full-scale onslaught against truth and the Judeo-Christian values in America like you have never seen before. We are truly living in a time described by Isaiah, where we have those who "call evil good, and good evil; that put darkness for light, and light for darkness; that put bitter for sweet, and sweet for bitter." (Isaiah 5:20, KJV). Finally, Paul tells us "But God shows his anger from heaven against all sinful, wicked people who suppress the truth by their wickedness." (Romans 1:18, NLT)

These are the same people who pretend to be wise, to follow the science, to be caring, inclusive, and respectful of others' beliefs and opinions, yet all the while cancelling and silencing those who don't agree with them or support and affirm their wickedness and lies. Paul tells us, that "Although they claimed to be wise, they became fools." (Romans 1:22, NIV) "Furthermore, just as they did not think it worthwhile to retain the knowledge of God, so God gave them over to a depraved mind, so that they do what ought not to be done." (Romans 1:28, NIV)

Ultimately, Paul warned that those who reject the love of the truth would become delusional. "And for this cause God shall send them strong delusion, that they should believe a lie." (2 Thessalonians 2:11 KJV)

ALL TRUTH IS GOD'S TRUTH

The thing about truth is that it has the same powerful and positive effect regardless as to whom or what source it comes from. Many people value truth based on its origin or the vehicle through which it comes. Thus, to them, truth is only as powerful as the source through which it comes and the manner it is presented. The truth is and the truth has its own inherent power regardless of its origin or manner of delivery. Truth can be found in many sources. While truth can be found in science, religion, and philosophy, truth can also be found in the educated and uneducated, the old man and the child, the rich and the poor. One of the errors we make is that we place a value on truth based on the source. For example, while I agree that the ministers of Christ should live godly, holy, and sanctified lives, I do not agree that one should reject their message, even if they are not living such a life, if their message is scripture-based or otherwise consistent with scripture. In fact, it was Jesus that said, regarding the religious leaders of His day, "The teachers of the law and the Pharisees sit in Moses' seat. So, you must be careful to do everything they tell you. But do not do what they do, for they do not practice what they preach." (Matthew 23:2-3, NIV)

Let's say that you are on the seventh floor of a hotel room, and you happen to look out of your window and see a person who is disheveled, stumbling and wobbling from side to side as he crosses the street. You see that this person is clearly drunk from alcohol, looking up at you and pointing straight ahead and yelling, "Fire, fire, fire!" to indicate that there is a fire in the lower part of the building that you are in. You have a choice to ignore him because he is drunk, disheveled, stumbling and wobbling as he walks, or you can, at the least, check out what he is yelling about. We might have a tendency to write such a person off simply because they are drunk. The point is, a message should never be rejected or accepted solely based on the source from which it comes, but on the verity of the message.

(Entwistle 2010) "All truth is ultimately under God's sovereignty." (p. 148)

Some truths are more valuable than other truths. For example, to be told that it's raining outside when you have no plans to go outside and will not in any way be negatively impacted by the rain is not as valuable as being told that a bridge is out on a road that you are traveling down at a speed of seventy miles per hour. To be made aware of the latter truth could save your life.

We have things that are scientifically true, and we have things that are biblically or theologically true. Are scientific truths more valuable, more important than biblical truths, or vice versa? To be honest, some scientific truths are more valuable than certain biblical truths. For example, to discover that it was unclean hands and other things in hospitals that were the primary reasons for the spread of infections in hospitals that led to thousands getting sick and dying is more important than being told that Gideon "...had threescore, and ten (seventy) sons of his body begotten: for he had many wives." (Judges 8:30) I am positing that the importance of a particular truth is ultimately determined by its benefit and outcome. So, I am not saying that it is not important to know about how many sons Gideon had. There is a reason why it is written. Let me further confess that as a sin-infected human being, with very limited knowledge and understanding, we don't always understand or appreciate the value of certain biblical truths. Yet, I think that I can carefully and fearfully conclude that there are some scientific truths that are more relevant to us today than some of the biblical history of antiquity. For example, if the world never knew about how many sons Gideon had, it wouldn't make much of a difference, if at all, in anyone's quality of life, and certainly not their eternal destiny.

One may be okay with, or find my statement a bit more acceptable, if one understood the following statement made by (Entwistle, 2010) as he states, "From God's perspective, all truth fits together cohesively." He goes on to say, "Nonetheless, if something is true, it cannot contradict other things that are true. This does not mean, however, that all truths are equally important." Entwistle also states, "...all truth is God's truth, so that wherever and however truth is discovered, its author is God." (p. 148-149)

Yet, let me categorically state, the most valuable and most important truths can be found exclusively in the Word of God which is recorded in the Judeo-Christian Bible. While truths about this life are important, truths about our eternal destiny and how we get there, whether it be eternal separation from God or eternal life with God and all that is related to these destinations, are by far the most important of all truths that can be known and accepted. Jesus informs us of this in many of His messages. In one place He asked the question, "And what do you benefit if you gain the whole world but lose your own soul? Is anything worth more than your soul?" (Matthew 16:26, NLT) In a couple of other places, as He compares our eternal destiny to this life, He says "Don't be afraid of those who want to kill your body; they cannot touch your soul. Fear only God, who can destroy both soul and body in hell." (Matthew 10:18, NLT) Finally, Jesus tells us, "Beware! Guard against every kind of greed. Life is not measured by how much you own." (Luke 12:15, NLT) These are timeless truths that cannot be observed in a microscope, seen with a telescope, detected by a radar or satellite, or ever discovered by the greatest of scientists, engineers, or philosophers, but divine truths that were only made known through the scriptures of truth. The most important things of life have never been known and will never be known except "... what is noted in the scripture of truth..." As was revealed to Daniel, "But I will shew thee that which is noted in the scripture of truth:" (Daniel 10:21, KJV)

As it relates to truth, "God is the author of all truth." (Entwistle, 2010, p. 150). It was John Calvin that said, "A dog barks when his master is attacked. I would be a coward if I saw that God's truth is attacked and yet would remain silent."

THINGS YOU SHOULD KNOW ABOUT THE TRUTH

God is "...a God of truth and without iniquity, just and right is he. (Deuteronomy 32:4, KJV)

All the works of God are done in truth (Psalms 33:4, KJV)

God's truth is a shield and buckler (Psalms 91:4, KJV)

The person who speaketh the truth sheweth forth righteousness (Proverbs 12:17, KJV)

No lie is of the truth. (1 John 2:21, KJV)

He that doeth truth, cometh to the light so that his deeds may be made known (John 3:21, KJV)

The truth will make you free. (John 8:32, KJV)

There is no truth in the devil. John 8:44, KJV)

Jesus is the way, the truth, and the life: no man cometh to the Father, but by me. (John 14:6, KJV)

God's word is truth (John 17:17, KJV)

People will become your enemy simply because you tell them the truth. (Galatians 4:16, KJV)

The way of truth is evil spoken of. (2 Peter 2:2, KJV)

If something is true, it will never contradict something else that is also true (Entwistle, 2010).

A PRAYER FOR TRUTH

"Lead me in thy truth, and teach me: for thou art the God of my salvation; on thee do I wait all the day. O send out thy light and thy truth: let them lead me; let them bring me unto thy holy hill, and to thy tabernacles. And take not the word of truth utterly out of my mouth; for I have hoped in thy judgments." (Psalms 25:5, 43:3 & 119:43, KJV)

THE DEVELOPMENT
OF A WORLDVIEW

According to Henley (2019), psychologist Alfred Adler believed, "The first invention of meaning in a person's life, then, is the creation of a worldview. Once a worldview develops, the child ponders how to live in the world as he or she perceives it. The child begins to plan his or her future by creating what Adler called "guiding fictions." These are future goals that are reasonable, given the child's worldview. If the worldview is positive, the child might attempt to embrace the world by planning to become a physician, scientist, artist, or teacher, for example. If the worldview is negative, the child might aggress toward the world by planning a life of crime and destruction." (p.513)

"From the worldview come guiding fictions (future goals), and from guiding fictions comes a lifestyle. Primarily, a lifestyle encompasses the everyday activities performed while pursuing one's goals. However, a person's lifestyle also determines which aspects of life are focused on, what is perceived and what is ignored, and how problems are solved." (Henley, 2019, p. 519)

WHAT IS A BIBLICAL WORLDVIEW?

A biblical worldview is a view of the world from a biblical perspective. It's a view of the world through the lens of the Bible. A biblical worldview is having a view of the world and all that pertains to the world, past, present, and future, based on what the Bible specifically states, implies, or otherwise indicates.

A biblical worldview is our view of life, the world and all related issues that inform our behavior, our thinking, our feelings, attitudes, dispositions, hopes, dreams, motivations, choices, decisions, opinions, and values. When we embrace a biblical worldview, all those issues are informed by what the Bible teaches.

CATEGORICAL REJECTION OF DISCRIMINATION AND CANCELLATION

Having a biblical world view does not cause one to mistreat, disrespect, hate, despise, be jealous of, envy, act maliciously towards, talk negatively about, engage in name calling, devalue, dislike, harm, demean, or otherwise treat another person wrong. A biblical world view respects other people's rights and freedoms of choice to live any kind of life or lifestyle they choose, notwithstanding, recognizing that there are divine consequences for the choices we make and the life we live. In addition, our choices and decisions are also limited or otherwise impacted by our constitution and the laws that are made that are consistent with said constitution.

A biblical worldview does not discriminate or in any way support discrimination against any person based on any reason including but not limited to the following:

- Race
- Color
- Religion or creed
- National origin or ancestry
- Sex (including gender, pregnancy, sexual orientation, and gender identity)
- Age
- Familial status
- Physical or mental disability
- Veteran status
- Genetic information
- Citizenship

Contrary to what most people think, including some believers and most unbelievers, a biblical worldview encourages all who embrace such a worldview to love everyone in both word and in deed, to be kind, tenderhearted, forgiving, merciful, gracious, longsuffering, temperate, gentle, considerate, compassionate and loving towards everyone without regards to their race, color, religion or creed, national origin or ancestry, sex, including gender, pregnancy, sexual orientation, or gender identity, age, physical or mental disability, veteran status, genetic information or citizenship.

NON-DISCRIMINATION DOES NOT MEAN AGREEMENT OR APPROVAL

Nonetheless, having a biblical worldview does not mean agreeing with everything everyone else does and believes. Having a biblical worldview means the person who holds such a worldview will disagree with and disapprove of any behavior, practice, lifestyle, philosophy, political position and dogma that is inconsistent with the written word of God as recorded in the Judeo- Christian Bible.

A BIBLICAL WORLDVIEW
PROHIBITS THE SUPPORT OF
ANTI-CHRISTIAN PRINCIPLES
AND VALUES

When one holds and lives by a biblical worldview, one cannot in any way support any lifestyle that is contrary to the teachings of the Bible. Neither can one encourage, engage in, participate in, or in any way promote or help others to promote such a lifestyle. That essentially means that being true to a biblical worldview prohibits one who holds a biblical worldview from marching in support of, signing petitions, voting for, or otherwise supporting those who overtly support or promise to promote such a lifestyle in any way.

LOVE AND DISAPPROVAL
ARE NOT ANTITHETICAL

A person who embraces a biblical worldview understands the importance of differentiating between the person and the person's behavior, as God does. God loves everyone unconditionally, sinners and unbelievers included, but God hates sin. While God hates all sins, and vehemently hates and detests certain sins more than others, He loves the sinner. Believers are asked to love each other as God loves them and to love others they encounter as they love themselves. Believers are commanded to love those they disagree with and those who disagree with us. Believers are to love everyone, even their enemies. Thus, as God loves people and disapproves of their behaviors, sometimes vehemently, those who hold and are guided by a biblical worldview are too commanded to love the person but to disapprove of behaviors that are contrary to a Judeo-Christian worldview. We are called to reject in practice and in principle all behavior that is antithetical to Christian principles. Practically speaking, this means we show acts of kindness and love towards everyone.

DSM, THE EVER-EVOLVING PSYCHIATRIC BIBLE

Since 1952 there have been eight publications of the Diagnostic and Statistical Manual by the American Psychiatric Association, including two revised versions. In 1968 when the Diagnostic and Statistical Manual of Mental Disorders 2nd Edition (DSM II), was prepared by The Committee On Nomenclature and Statistics of The American Psychiatric Association and published by the American Psychiatric Association, homosexuality was listed as one of the mental disorders categorized as "Sexual deviations." American Psychiatric Association (APA, 1968)

According to the *DSM II*, these disorders were among the disorders classified as personality disorders. After pushback from various groups over the years, there were several attempts to rename and reclassify homosexuality to include such names as sexual orientation disorder and ego dystonic homosexuality. Eventually the term disappears from any category of sex-related disorder and morphed into gender identity disorder and currently gender dysphoria. It is interesting to note that these changes were not based exclusively, if at all, on new scientific evidence but on pushback from certain individuals and groups, cultural changes, and cultural norms. The aforementioned changes were later arguably accepted and published because of a majority vote of certain constituents, pressured by certain special interest groups, individuals and politics, and in some cases in opposition of many in the psychiatric community.

When I was studying for my various degrees, including my clinical studies, the need for fidelity to evidence based practices and the reliance on empirically sound and peer reviewed conclusions were the required standard of expectation regarding treatment and practice. However, today, regarding LGBTQ ideology, particularly gender identity, homosexuality and transgenderism, there does not appear to be the same call. Rather, today, evidence based practices, empirically sound and peer reviewed conclusions appear to give way to cultural norms based on the subjective feelings, emotions, and desires of a very small percentage of our population and raised to a cultural norm that is deemed worthy of being pushed on the majority of the population who are not members of that culture, and does not see or accept this behavior as normal but deviant.

Major life altering decisions are being made, not based on the "science," but by politicians, educators, judges, elected and unelected officials, doctors who have cast off their oath to "Do no harm," special interest groups, based on cultural norms and a majority vote of a populace. There was a time in our nation, that, before a judge would make a major judicial decision regarding a medical issue, that judge, if he was fair and making his decisions based on the facts, uninfluenced by politics, would hear from both sides regarding the issue and make the best-informed decision he could, based on the evidence presented.

Today a child as young as three or four years old can subjectively claim to be virtually any sex or gender they want to be solely based on their inner sense, desire, preferences, feelings or the influence of parents or others. For example, a person may claim to be non-binary and report that they are in fact neither male or female, boy or girl. Another person may claim to be gender diverse, which indicates that this individual identifies as having multiple genders or no gender at all. In either case, very young children are allowed and encouraged to make such nonsensical claims with no empirical evidence to support them. Science told us for many years that children were incapable of making major decisions regarding their health, education, legal issues or any other major issues regarding their overall safety and wellbeing or life and death. All that has been cast aside. The only factors to be considered today are their feelings, which the DMS acknowledge can, in certain cases, be a mental disorder.

As late as 2000 when the *Diagnostic and Statistical Manual of Mental Disorders*, Fourth Edition, Text Revision also known as the DSM-IV-TR, was published, it reported that "having strong and persistent feelings of discomfort with one's assigned sex, the desire to possess the body of the opposite sex, and the desire to be regarded by others as a member of the other sex" was considered to be a disorder identified as gender identity disorder. American Psychological Association (APA, 2000)

Approximately 13 years later, the Fifth Edition of the *Diagnostic and Statistical Manual of Mental Disorders*, also referred to as the DSM-5, was published and the term "gender dysphoria" replaces the term "gender identity disorder." According to the DSM-5, the term "gender dysphoria" "...is more descriptive than the previous DSM-IV terms gender identity disorder and focusses on dysphoria as the clinical problem, not identity per se." American Psychiatric Association (APA, 2013)

According to the DSM-5, the diagnostic criteria for gender dysphoria is as follows:

"A marked incongruence between one's experience/ expressed gender and assigned gender, or at least 6 months' duration, as manifested by at least six of the following (one of which must be Criterion A1):

1. A strong desire to be rid of one's primary and/or secondary sex characteristics because of a marked incongruence with one's experienced/expressed gender (or in young adolescents, a desire to prevent the development of the anticipated secondary sex characteristics)

2. In boys (assigned gender), a strong preference for cross-dressing or simulating female attire; or in girls (assigned gender), a strong preference for wearing only typical masculine clothing and a strong resistance to the wearing of typical feminine clothing.

3. A strong preference for cross-gender roles in make-believe play or fantasy play.

4. A strong preference for the toys, games, or activities stereotypically used or engaged in by the other gender.

5. A strong preference for playmates of the other gender.

6. In boys (assigned gender), a strong rejection of typically masculine toys, games and activities and a strong avoidance of rough-and-tumble play; or in girls (assigned gender), a strong rejection of typically feminine toys, games, and activities.

7. A strong dislike of one's sexual anatomy.

8. A strong desire for the primary and/or secondary sex characteristics that match one's experienced gender." American Psychiatric Association (APA, 2013)

The information listed herein is not listed a means to provide guidance and directions in the diagnosis of any mental disorder. The information is listed solely for informational purposes and to show what is listed regarding the diagnostic criteria. Please notice that the criteria for meeting the diagnosis for both gender identity disorder and gender dysphoria are replete with terms such as "strong and persistent, intense desire, strong preference, repeatedly stated desire, insistence, fantasies, marked incongruence, make believe, strong rejection and strong dislike." Every one of these terms are associated with our emotions and our spirits.

Each is also dynamic and subjective. Unlike the biological factors such as the color of a person's skin and their biological make up, each of these characteristics are also influenced by numerous external and internal factors, including but not limited to mental illness and satanic lies and influences. Often times many older people who report that they have these experiences also report that, at some point in their lives, they were molested or raped by someone of the same or opposite sex, or otherwise abused and traumatized. It is not ours to deny that one feels the way one purports to feel. Neither is it ours to deny one's belief about whom they think they are or want to be.

For the diagnostic criteria for adolescents and adults, please see the DSM-5 or the latest publication.

Finally, there were additional diagnostic updates and changes in the DSM in 2022. According to the DSM-5-TR-5, the text of gender dysphoria was updated to use culturally sensitive language, e.g., "desired gender" was changed to "experienced gender," "cross-sex medical procedure" was updated to "gender affirming medical procedure," "cross-sex hormone treatment' to "gender affirming hormone treatment," "natal male" to "individual assigned male at birth" and "natal female" to "individual assigned female at birth". Moreover, "differences in sex development" was noted to be an alternate term for "disorders of sex development." American Psychiatric Association (APA, 2022)

Unlike the DSMs, the truth presented in the word of God has not changed, has not evolved, has never been decided through any democratic process, special interest group or a majority of the votes of its constituents. God's Word contains no theories, no suppositions and no claims that are attributed to God, Christ, the Holy Spirit, or any of the angels of God that has been proven to be in error or is rebuttable. "Oh, the dept of the riches of the wisdom and knowledge of God! How unsearchable his judgments, and his paths beyond tracing out!" (Romans 11:33, NIV)

THE JUDEO-CHRISTIAN BIBLE

The Judeo-Christian Bible, when it maintains it fidelity to the original writings, has no truth or values that are included that are there because those truths or values were voted upon by a majority of any special interest group or constituents. For the sake of any critics, the revised versions of the Bible are not revisions of the truth of scripture but revisions of the translations. No one has a right to arbitrarily change anything God said. There is indubitably no statement of truth made by God, his Christ or the Holy Spirit regarding any of the issues of life, whether scientific or otherwise, that has changed or is remotely falsifiable. While God has changed His process and approach, He has never changed anything that He declared to be true at one time and later had to change it because He discovered it wasn't true. "God is not a man, so he does not lie. He is not human, so he does not change his mind." (Numbers 23:19, NLT)

We are encouraged to have great confidence in what God proclaims as truth for two reasons. First, He is not human, so He is not subject to human limitations. Humans are mortal and finite. God is immortal and infinite. Humans are limited in their knowledge and learn through a process of trial and error. God is omniscient. Second, "So God has given both his promise and his oath. These two things are unchangeable because it is impossible for God to lie." (Hebrews 6:18, NLT). "...God cannot lie..." (Titus 1:2 KJV) One of the many differences between God and scientists, the theories of science and biblical truth, is that science has made many errors in its predictions and claims of truth that turned out to be deadly wrong, whereas there is not a single word of truth of scripture, spoken by God, that has turned out to be erroneous. God does not postulate or offer theories, suppositions or anything that can be refutable or falsifiable.

"Who has measured the waters in the hollow of his hand,
or with the breadth of his hand marked off the heavens?
Who has held the dust of the earth in a basket,
or weighed the mountains on the scales.
and the hills in a balance?
Who can fathom the Spirit of the LORD,
or instruct the LORD as his counselor?
Whom did the LORD consult to enlighten him,
and who taught him the right way?
Who was it that taught him knowledge,
or showed him the path of understanding?"
(Isaiah 40:12-14, NIV)

"...Believe in the Lord your God, and you shall be established; believe His prophets, and you shall prosper."
(2 Chronicles 20:20, NKJB)

WHERE IS THE SCIENCE?

One may ask, where is the science? Not to say that science would therefore make the theories, suppositions and conclusions posited by the DSM regarding LGBTQ claims or any other group or individual who speaks in the name of science any more credible or true, especially if they contradict the teachings of scripture. It was psychologist Karl Popper who stated that, "A scientific theory must be refutable." (Henley, 2019, p.9).

Popper further suggested that risky predictions are a prerequisite of scientific theories. Popper also stated, "The highest status that a scientific explanation can have is "not yet disconfirmed." (Henley 2019). Popper saw scientific truth as being dynamic and falsification of many scientific theories as highly common and expected. The very sad part about any science, or other individuals or groups who are pushing the LGBTQ and Transgender agenda, is, being wrong about transgenderism, especially the hormone treatments, surgical procedures and psychological impact, will result, in irreversible harm. There are already a number of people who have experienced these so-called "gender affirming treatments" that are suffering irreparable mental, emotional, and physical damage. However, those with an agenda don't want people to know about it. We cannot afford to get this wrong.

NON-BINARY GENDER
AND NON-BINARY SEX
IS A MISNOMER

The reality is, there are no gender diverse or non-binary gender or sex. Regarding gender, it is interesting to note that according to the DSM-V, "The need to introduce the term *gender* arose with the realization that for individuals with conflicting or ambiguous biological indicators of sex (i.e., "intersex"), the lived role in society and/or the identification as male or female could not be uniformly associated or predicted from the biological indicators and, later, that some individuals develop an identity as female or male at variance with their uniform set of classical biological indicators." American Psychiatric Association (2013) *Diagnostic and Statistical Manual of Mental Disorders* (5th ed.) America Psychiatric Association, Washington D.C. However, it appears that the term gender has evolved, as has many other things in the LGBTQ community. The claim that one's gender is fluid may be correct, but only in the imaginary sense, as gender is a term that was apparently invented to deal with a conflict between a person's biological indicators and how they have chosen to identify. People can change the way they identify as often as they choose. Yet, it is true, as it was stated by Edward de Bono, "Perception is real even when it is not reality." https://www.azquotes.com/author/1649-Edward_de_Bono/tag/perception

As such, subjectively speaking, there is no limit as to how one may choose to identify regarding their gender so long as we stick to a certain definition of the term. The confusion, and thus the problem, appears to be treating gender as if it is the same as biological sex, or as if gender has the same definition as sex, and denying biological sex.

Historically speaking, the term gender is reported to have been linked to a psychologist by the name of John Money in 1955 during his controversial experiment with Mr. David Reimer. He is also reported to have been the first person to differentiate between gender and biological sex. John Money is also the person who is reported to, at the least, believe that gender identity was not an innate characteristic, but learned. Money reportedly further believed that gender identity was fluid and could be shaped and influenced by environmental factors and behavioral interventions. Money was the controversial psychologist who attempted to trans David Reimer, who was born as an identical twin boy, into living as a female from a child after a surgery that went terribly wrong. Reimer is believed to have been eight years old at the time. Dr. Money was unsuccessful in his attempt to trans Mr. Reimer, who was born a male. Eventually Mr. Reimer reportedly committed suicide, as he was never able to trans from the male he was to the female Dr. Money attempted to trans him to. It is reported that through all the biological changes made to his physical body, all the efforts to force him to live as a female, there was, in fact, a strong incongruence between his desires, his interests, his feelings, his emotions, and his preferences between who he had been transed to become and who he was biologically from conception and from birth. One has to wonder how many David Reimers are in our world who, for one reason or another, have been transed from an early age and who are now experiencing this strong incongruence between their actual biological sex and the gender that they have been transed to. The story regarding John Money and David Reimer is retrieved from https://www.spiked-online.com/2023/02/05/dr-john-money-and-the-sinister-origins-of-gender-ideology/..

In our contemporary culture, contrary to the original definition of gender, today gender is treated to be virtually the same as sex in the sense that gender is considered to be innate and as static and immutable as biological sex. However, that appears to be scientifically and historically incorrect, as gender is not innate but a social construct, where people learn to act in accordance with certain socially constructed expectations. So, if, when a person says they are non-binary, and they are referring to their gender, don't argue with them; rather, let them have their belief or claim. However, you are not therefore also accepting the false notion that a person can be non-binary regarding their biological sex or gender diverse as to their biological sex, even though they claim to be so. In fact, the etymology of the word gender literally means type, kind, or sort. It is physically and scientifically impossible to be sexually non-binary.

Objectively speaking, every human being is categorically male or female based on their birth and consistent with their biological and physiological sex characteristics. Changing one's physiological features by getting an operation, dressing like the opposite sex, getting hormone treatment, thinking and acting like the opposite sex, feeling like the opposite sex, or having desires for the same sex, does not change the fact that a person is either male or female based on their sex at birth. One can never become a different sex simply by changing behavior or appearances. There is no operation that can change a person's gender, as gender is not biological. Neither is there an operation that can change a person's biological sex, because biological sex is an intricately woven, intrinsically connected, innate and indivisible set of characteristics that makes a person male or female. The whole of what it means to be a male or female is wrapped up in conception. Exchanging parts, getting rid of parts, modifying parts, enhancing parts, or doing any other thing to change the way a person looks does not effectively change that person from being a male to a female or vice versa. People may change the way they identify, the way they look, the way they act and behave, but they are not able to effectively change their biological sex.

Sex refers to "the different biological and physiological characteristics of males and females, such as reproductive organs, chromosomes, hormones, etc." Gender refers to "the socially constructed characteristics of women and men – such as norms, roles and relationships of and between groups of women and men. Retrieved from: https://www.coe.int/en/web/gender-matters/sex-and-gender

But from the beginning of the creation, God "made them male and female." (Mark 10:6, NKJV.)

SEX IS DETERMINED
AT CONCEPTION

Sex is determined at conception by genes that are contained within chromosomes, as numerous other biological and physiological characteristics are. For example, I have heard people posit that men have a missing rib because God removed one of Adam's ribs. Common knowledge and science will prove that is incorrect. Making a physiological change to Adam's body did not impact his genes. The appearance of Adam's offspring was not based on Adam's outward appearance or the operation performed on him to remove one of his ribs, but his genetic makeup. Adam would always produce people who have the same biological and physiological characteristics as he did in his original creation.

Not only is sex determined at conception, but more importantly and succinctly put, males and females' sex are determined at conception, and confirmed by ultrasounds as they develop, and ultimately at birth. Regarding the birth of several people listed in the Bible, including Jesus, their sex was, for the sake of this writing, determined at conception. "And behold, thy cousin Elisabeth, she hath also conceived a son in her old age: and this is the sixth month with her, who was called barren" (Luke 1:36, KJV). The key phrase in this verse is "conceived a son." Here, the angel tells Mary just as she will conceive a son, her cousin Elisabeth has already conceived a son. Male and female is determined at conception. "Therefore the Lord himself shall give you a sign; Behold, a virgin shall conceive, and bear a son, and shall call his name Immanuel." (Isaiah 7:14, KJV) "And behold, thou shalt conceive in thy womb, and bring forth a son, and shalt call his name JESUS" (Luke 1:31, KJV). I say for the sake of this writing, because people's purpose and ultimate destiny is determined long before they are conceived, a person does not become or evolve into a male or female. A person is conceived a male or female.

Regarding the sex of an individual being determined at birth, the Bible describes it as a two-step process which is conception and bringing forth or birth. The word determine has several synonyms, a few of which are decide, settle, resolve or rule. So, whether a person is male or female or a boy or a girl, is decided, settled, resolved and ruled to be so, at conception. It is a human being from conception, and as such, is either a male or a female, a son or daughter, a boy or girl at conception, not after the doctor sees his or her genitals. The genitals are only further evidence of whether a person is a male or female. I have listed a few additional scriptures below for your review and consideration regarding conceiving and bearing a son:

"And the angel of the LORD appeared unto the woman, and said unto her, Behold now, thou art barren, and bearest not: but thou shalt, conceive and bear a son." (Judges 13:3, KJV)

"For, lo, thou shalt, conceive and bear a son; and no razor shall come on his head: for the child shall be a Nazarite unto God from the womb: and he shall begin to deliver Israel out of the hand of the Philistines." (Judges 13:5, KJV)

Notice, the process is first the conception of a male or a female; subsequently, when the child is brought to full term, he or she is brought forth or birthed. But for the nine months from conception, it's a growing boy or girl a growing male or female. Not at any point along the way is the child non-gender, gender diverse, non-binary, gender neutral or anything other than male or female unless there is a deformity. Otherwise, there are no changes from that which was originally conceived.

Nothing happens between conception and birth except growth and development as it is fashioned by God. Solomon stated, "As thou knowest not what is the way of the spirit, nor how the bones do grow in the womb of her that is with child: even so thou knowest not the works of God who maketh all." (Ecclesiastes 11:5 KJV) The spirit of man, that is given by God and comes from God, is given at conception. James tells us, "For as the body without the spirit is dead..." (James 2:26 KJV). It was

Job that said, "Did not he that made me in the womb make him? And did not one fashion us in the womb?" (Job 31:15 KJV)

"Before I formed thee in the belly I knew thee; and before thou camest forth out of the womb I sanctified thee..." (Jeremiah 1:5 KJV). Finally, male and female are a divine formation of God. Each is formed differently and from different substance. Man came from the dust and woman came from the man.

While each sex has more or less of one hormone or the other, increasing the hormone levels in one does not change one's sex to the opposite sex. It simply becomes a case where one sex has more of a certain hormone than normal and natural. This process will also alter the natural growth and development of the male or female. Yet, no matter how one alters the biological makeup of a person who is born male or female, one cannot trans into being another sex. Sex is more than desire, likes, interest, preferences, perspective, concepts, hormones, appearances, self-identification, or feelings. Sex is a comprehensive set of factors that are biopsychosocial and spiritual. Males and females think, feel, process information, perceive, act, react, think, and love consistent with their biological sex. Male and female also have an internal biological and physiological make up and processes that does not change with feelings, desires, and external changes. Females normally and naturally have breasts, produce milk, have ovaries that produce ova, (eggs), have fallopian tubes, a uterus, a certain size of a brain and is naturally pierced. Males normally do not have breasts, lactate or otherwise produce enough milk to nourish a child. It is also believed that if and when a man lactates, it's abnormal and may be due to some underlying medical problem, or otherwise as a result of medication or other substance introduced to the man's body. Neither do men, by nature, have fallopian tubes, a uterus or produce eggs. Man also is said to have a larger brain and is not pierced. You can add many more differences between a male and a female.

Having sexual desire or sexual attraction for the same sex

makes you no more that sex than having sexual attraction or desire for an animal makes you an animal. While being a male and female is a very static condition, desires, including sexual desires, are not. Sexual desire can, and is, influenced by many factors. Sexual desire can be natural or unnatural. Sexual desire can be normal or abnormal. Not only is there a long history of males and females having sexual desires for the same sex, but men and women have a history of uncontrolled sexual desires including having strong sexual desire for and engaging in sex with animals, having sexual attraction and engaging in sex with children, having an attraction and engaging in sex with dead bodies (also known as necrophilia, or sexual intercourse with, or attraction towards corpses), having strong sexual attractions and engaging in sexual activities with their own children, siblings, step-children, various objects and self-manipulation. These are just additional reasons why a person's sexual desire should never be used to inform their gender, or otherwise as a determinant factor as to whether they are male or female. Sexual desire is biologically, physiologically, psychologically, socially, spiritually and, as noted before, environmentally and culturally influenced. This influence may be positive or negative, healthy or unhealthy, good or bad, morally right or wrong. Having homosexual desires is only determinative of one thing, and that is the influences behind the desire and the type and dynamic nature and impact of the desire.

"Now the works of the flesh are evident, which are: adultery, fornication, uncleanness, lewdness," (Galatians 5:19 NKJV) "When you follow the desires of your sinful nature, the results are very clear: sexual immorality, impurity, lustful pleasures..." (Galatians 5:19 NLT)

HOMOSEXUALITY IS NEITHER GENETICALLY CONCEIVED, CARRIED, BORN OR REPRODUCED

Homosexuality is not only not genetically carried or reproduced, it's impossible to do so. Two men and two women are incapable of "reproducing" or producing, not only after their kind, but at all. The only other possible scenario that could be hypothesized would be a homosexual man and a homosexual woman having a child. In such a case, if homosexuals could produce, or reproduce after their kind, they would, by a significant probability, produce homosexual children, because parents pass on certain traits or characteristics to their children and these children inherit these genetically transferred traits. I know of no science that supports such a hypothesis. Even if one did, a biblical worldview would show that such a hypothesis is simply that, a hypothesis.

Another factor to consider about homosexuality: while proponents of homosexuality want you to think that having homosexual desires are inherent, genetic, and therefore immutable and unchangeable, statistics show that in places where homosexuality is more accepting, the population of those who embrace this lifestyle and become homosexuals is higher. In addition, there are significant recruitment efforts, including the proselytizing of young and vulnerable children to become homosexuals. These efforts are being carried out in the name of healthcare, acceptance, gender-affirming care and support, but are really just a deceptive and very aggressive effort to push the homosexual agenda on society and to convert more people to the homosexual lifestyle and the acceptance of that lifestyle. Homosexuality is not growing by way of natural production or reproduction but by way of indoctrination, recruitment and influence from various individuals, groups, organizations, the news media, social media, politicians, educators, governmental edicts, and other factors. One of the most dangerous practices of today is so called "gender-affirming care" which may include everything from affirming a person's name and desired pronouns to body-altering drugs and surgical interventions that may include amputations of breasts and genitals.

The practice of homosexuality is not right or wrong based on how many people believe it's right or wrong, how many people support it, laws that are passed to sanction it or to punish those who speak against it. Homosexuality is wrong because God says it's wrong and it's impossible for God to lie, though one may attempt to suppress the truth of God and to turn the truth of God into a lie.

One may argue that there are some human beings who are androgynous or hermaphroditic who have both male and female genitals and therefore they should be able to choose which sex they want to be identified as. While it is true that there are people, though a small percentage generally, that are either male or female who may have multiple genitals including genitals that are of the opposite sex, other characteristics will further determine and define whether that person is male or female. These conditions are not normal and may be, in some cases caused by medication, or some other biological malfunction. Yet, if the person has male and female genitals but also has ovaries, breasts, is pierced, and can conceive and birth a child, the person is a female. On the other hand, if the person has male and female genitals, but none of the other characteristics of a female, the person is a male. Yet, this is not the case for an overwhelming majority of people who identify as homosexuals or transgender. Most people who want to identify as homosexuals, transgender, nonbinary, or other members of the LGBTQ community, overwhelmingly and distinctively have all the physiological and biological features of one or the other sex.

Nevertheless, having sexual characteristics that may be

inconsistent with other characteristics is a result of sin and not normal. Biological malfunctions and all other types of biological abnormalities are a result of sin. We live in a sin-cursed world, and many things go wrong during the conception, reproduction and birth process. There are conditions where people are born joined together (conjoined) at various points on their bodies, born without certain organs, without eyes, without a brain, without one or more kidneys, and many other birth defects. The fact of their abnormal birth does not make them any less human. They are human beings with some level of abnormality in their birth. So is a male or female born with more than one genital; they are either male or female with an abnormal birth.

Finally, those who argue and promote the belief that homosexuality is genetic, it is further argued that since homosexuality is genetic, it is not a choice but an innate and immutable condition. Therefore, those who identify with and practice homosexuality are behaving in a manner consistent with their true selves and should not be expected to change, nor should they be encouraged to change through any therapeutic, religious, or other intervention.

THE DELUSIONAL
DIFFERENTIATION

In our current world and culture, a person who claims to be gender diverse, non-binary or transgender can never be seen or thought of as being delusional. Yet, according to the *Diagnostic and Statistical Manual* (DSM), there are those who make such claims of being a sex or gender that is different from their biological sex or sex at birth, who are in fact delusional. Yet, there are laws that prevent subjecting anyone who make such claims to therapy. Furthermore, society as a whole, including Christians, are called upon to affirm such behavior in all who make such claims without the liberty to consider that some are in fact delusional and suffering from a mental disorder. For example, conversion therapy is legally banned in twenty-two states. It is truly nonsensical to categorically ban a treatment for a mental health condition that in reality does exist.

Admittedly, there are LGBTQ and Transgender claims that are in fact delusional and thus are a result of a mental disorder. The DSM-IV-TR stated that, "Insistence by a person with a gender identity disorder that he or she is of the other sex is not considered a delusion, because what is invariably meant is that the person feels like a member of the other sex rather than truly believes that he or she is a member of the other sex." American Psychiatric Association (APA, 2000) Here, it appears that the previous conclusion drawn by the American Psychological Association was the differentiation between what the person felt and what they really believed. This appears to suggest that if a person who is a male truly believed that he was a female, he was delusional and was suffering from a mental disorder. In the updated DSM-V, this same organization made changes to their conclusion. In the DSM-V, it is stated that "In the absence of psychotic symptoms, insistence by an individual with gender dysphoria that he or she is of some other gender is not considered a delusion." American Psychiatric Association (APA, 2013)

The language is interesting to say the least, as it does not make a distinction between whether this insistence is based on a person's feeling versus whether they truly believe that he or she is a member of the opposite sex. However, the DSM-IV-TR states, "... Schizophrenia and severe Gender Identity Disorder may coexist." American Psychiatric Association (APA, 2000). Additionally, the DSM V states, Schizophrenia (or other psychotic disorders) and gender dysphoria may co-occur." American Psychiatric Association (APA, 2013)

So, both conclude that "Schizophrenia (or other psychotic-disorders) may be present in certain gender identity disorder and gender dysphoria claims. American Psychiatric Association (APA, 2000, 2013). How then can anyone who care about the Homosexual, transgender and other members of the LGBTQ+ community unilaterally and exclusively criminalize those who attempt to provide counseling and therapy for these individuals.

JESUS AND HOMOSEXUALITY
JESUS ONLY RECOGNIZES TWO
SEXES (MALE AND FEMALE)

Regarding sex and gender, Jesus only mentioned and emphatically identified two sexes and genders, which are male and female, even though Jesus recognizes that man may make biological changes to themselves, such as a man becoming a eunuch. While Jesus acknowledges that a man may become a eunuch, He does not therefore also deny the sex of the individual, only that he may intentionally choose to be neutered. it doesn't change his sex. It only affects his sexual desire by reducing the man's biological ability to produce testosterone, sperm formation, sexual behavior and sexual interest. Aging may have the same or similar effects. Yet, a eunuch is either a male or female. There is no trans into being a different sex or gender from their biological sex with which they were born.

SEX AND "GENDER" ARE EXCLUSIVELY BIOLOGICAL

Jesus further shared His position regarding sex and indicated that sex and gender, if and when it is referred to as sex, is a biological and physiological aspect of the human experience. When Jesus spoke regarding marriage, He revealed that marriage and sex are human and thus earthly experience. This position also indicates, categorically, that sex is biological.

Sex and "gender" differentiation are mortal and corruptible characteristics of the human experience.

That same day Jesus was approached by some Sadducees—religious leaders who say there is no resurrection from the dead. They posed this question: "Teacher, Moses said, 'If a man dies without children, his brother should marry the widow and have a child who will carry on the brother's name.' Well, suppose there were seven brothers. The oldest one married and then died without children, so his brother married the widow. But the second brother also died, and the third brother married her. This continued with all seven of them. Last of all, the woman also died. So, tell us, whose wife will she be in the resurrection? For all seven were married to her.' Jesus replied, 'your mistake is that you don't know the Scriptures, and you don't know the power of God. For when the dead rise, they will neither marry nor be given in marriage. In this respect they will be like the angels in heaven." (Matthew 22:23-30, NLT)

While Jesus's statement is clear and unambiguous, the totality of what He is saying has to be understood by implication. The believers' resurrected bodies will be like those of angels. We know several things about angels. One thing that is clear about angels is that they are spiritual beings. In speaking of the angels, Hebrews 1:7 KJV says, "He makes his angels spirits, and his servants flames of fire." "Who makes His angels spirits, His ministers a flame of fire" (Psalms 104:4 KJV.) Though angels appear in the form of mortal men, they are not men, mortal, or human.

By implication, Jesus is telling us that when people are raised from the dead, they will not have any earthly, biological, or physiological characteristics of a sexual nature. Another implication that is apparent here is that while sexual desires may be spiritually influenced, male and female sex is not spiritual but physical. Human sex is not metaphysical or discarnate. No one is male and female in spirit or in any other metaphysical or discarnate way. Upon the resurrection there will not be flesh and blood and people will be asexual.

DID JESUS OMIT TEACHING AGAINST HOMOSEXUALITY?

Some argue that Jesus did not teach against homosexuality, thus suggesting that He did not have a problem with homosexuality because He never addressed it or spoke against it. That is incorrect. While Jesus never addressed or mentioned homosexuality directly, homosexuality is inclusive in a list of sexual sins known as fornication or illicit or illegal sexual acts. Fornication includes all sexual engagements between any two human beings that are not legally or culturally married to each other, or a human being engaging in sexual acts with any other animate or inanimate thing, and includes sex between humans, animals, inanimate objects, and people of the same sex whether they are legally married or not.

It is true, as some claim, that Jesus did not directly and explicitly teach against homosexuality. Yet, that doesn't mean that He did not teach against it. First, Jesus's audience consisted of people who knew the law and attempted to live according to the law. Therefore, He did not need to address the issue of homosexuality, or at the least spend much time on it, as His followers and those in the Jewish religion and culture were clear regarding the forbidden practice of homosexuality. There was a very serious prohibition against homosexuality, as there was against all sexual immorality and other sins. One of the reasons why homosexuality was not as big an issue as it is and was in the gentile world, or in our world today, is because God had put in place a strong deterrent to sexual immorality, including homosexuality. In addition, the Jewish people, in particular, were aware of how God dealt with sexual immorality, including the death of twenty-three thousand ((23,000) in one day and the impact of homosexuality in God's decision to totally overthrow and destroy Sodom and Gomorrah. It was clear that the law was in full force and effect during the time of Jesus, when He stated: "Do not think that I have come to abolish the Law or the Prophets; I have not come to abolish them but to fulfill them." (Matthew 5:17, NIV)

One cannot justify the practice of homosexuality and erroneously conclude that Jesus did not address it because it's not singled out. Not only did Jesus specifically not deal with homosexuality, but there were many other very important issues that He never referred to or specifically addressed while He was here. Teachings and concerns regarding many major doctrinal issues were deferred by Jesus and passed on to His apostles to be dealt with by them and other church leaders whom He ordained and would later call. In fact, Jesus told His disciples, "There is so much more I want to tell you, but you can't bear it now. When the Spirit of truth comes, he will guide you into all truth. He will not speak on his own but will tell you what he has heard. He will tell you about the future. He will bring me glory by telling you whatever he receives from me." (John 16:12-14, NLT)

JESUS ON HOMOSEXUAL MARRIAGE

Did Jesus address the issue of homosexual marriage? Yes! Jesus categorically proclaims marriage as the sexual union between a man and a woman. While there were some issues that Jesus did not explicitly deal with, there were others that He did address. One reason was not necessarily due to their importance or lack of importance, but because He was asked about it directly. Such is the case with marriage. Jesus was asked about marriage and divorce. This question afforded Jesus with the opportunity to share God's position regarding the topic, and subsequently, informs the rest of us of His position.

Jesus categorically states that God's plan and intention for marriage is for a male and female (man and a woman) to be joined together sexually. Jesus further explains and affirms that it is the sexual union between a male (man) and female (woman) that results in their becoming one flesh and effecting a marriage. Becoming one flesh is the ultimate result of marriage.

The concept of marriage, relative to who should and can be married and what makes a marriage, was originated, sanctioned, and blessed by God. Marriage is and was God's idea. God has not handed the institution of marriage over to man to change or, in any way, to modify. From the beginning of this divine institution, God proclaimed, "Therefore shall a man leave his father and his mother and shall cleave unto his wife: and they shall be one flesh." (Genesis 2:24, KJV)

Jesus did not change or modify God's original plan or process. In fact, Jesus appears to reaffirm it in a word for word reiteration and quotes what God originally stated, "And he answered and said unto them, Have ye not read, that he which made them at the beginning made them male and female. And said, For this cause shall a man leave father and mother, and shall cleave to his wife: and they twain shall be one flesh?

Wherefore they are no more twain, but one flesh. What therefore God hath joined together, let not man put asunder." (Matthew 19:4-6, KJV) The same reference to Jesus's response regarding this matter was also recorded by Mark (Mark, 10:6-9)

A BIBLICAL BASIS FOR BECOMING ONE FLESH

GENESIS 12:24

"That is why a man leaves his father and mother and is united to his wife, and they become one flesh." (Genesis 2:24, NIV)

"This explains why a man leaves his father and mother and is joined to his wife, and the two are united into one." (Genesis 2:24, NLT)

"Therefore shall a man leave his father and his mother and shall cleave unto his wife: and they shall be one flesh." (Genesis 2:24, KJV)

MATTHEW 19:5

"...and said, 'For this reason a man will leave his father and mother and be united to his wife, and the two will become one flesh.' (Matthew 19:5, NIV)

"And he said, 'This explains why a man leaves his father and mother and is joined to his wife, and the two are united into one.'"(Matthew 19:5, NLT)

"And said, For this cause shall a man leave father and mother, and shall cleave to his wife: and they twain shall be one flesh?" (Matthew 19:5, KJV)

MATTHEW 19:6

"So they are no longer two, but one flesh. Therefore, what God has joined together, let no one separate." (Matthew 19:6, NIV)

"Since they are no longer two but one, let no one split apart what God has joined together." (Matthew 19:6, NLT)

"Wherefore they are no more twain, but one flesh. What therefore God hath joined together, let not man put asunder." (Matthew 19:6, KJV)

"So then, they are no longer two but one flesh. Therefore, what God has joined together, let not man separate." (Matthew 19:6, NKJV)

MARK 10:8

"...and the two will become one flesh.' So they are no longer two, but one flesh." (Mark 10:8, NIV)

"...and the two are united into one.' Since they are no longer two but one," (Mark 10:8, NLT)

"And they twain shall be one flesh: so then they are no more twain, but one flesh." (Mark 10:8, KJV)

1 CORINTHIANS 6:16

"Do you not know that he who unites himself with a prostitute is one with her in body? For it is said, 'The two will become one flesh.'" (1 Corinthians 6:16, NIV)

"And don't you realize that if a man joins himself to a prostitute, he becomes one body with her? For the Scriptures say, 'The two are united into one.'" (1 Corinthians 6:16, NLT)

"What? know ye not that he which is joined to an harlot is one body? for two, saith he, shall be one flesh." (1 Corinthians 6:16, KJV).

EPHESIANS 5:31

"For this reason a man will leave his father and mother and be united to his wife, and the two will become one flesh." (Ephesians 5:31, NIV)

"As the Scriptures say, 'A man leaves his father and mother and is joined to his wife, and the two are united into one.'" (Ephesians 5:31, NLT)

"For this cause shall a man leave his father and mother, and shall be joined unto his wife, and they two shall be one flesh." (Ephesians 5:31, KJV)

JESUS AFFIRMS MALE AND FEMALE BECOMING ONE FLESH

Becoming one flesh is an exclusive ability of a male and female. The statement is not just a divine edict, it is a scientific proclamation. Why do I suggest this? I suggest this because the only two human beings who are capable of and would become one upon consummation are two human beings who began as one. Male and female becomes one because the female has her origin in the male. The female came out of the man. Females are literally bone of bone of the male. So, when the bone that was taken from the man is reunited to the man, sexually, in the form of a female or woman, she again becomes one flesh with the man from whom she was originally taken. This union, or reunion, is the essence of marriage. Thus, males uniting with males and females uniting with females doesn't accomplish this by any means imaginable. It requires a re-uniting and a uniting of a male and female. Other unions, though sexual, are ineffective in resulting in two people becoming one flesh. Thus, homosexuality is a human invention and institution that can never result in marriage. The true meaning of marriage is two human beings of the opposite sex becoming one flesh when they have sex with each other consistent with the legal or other authorized process by which people become married. The one flesh is an exclusive reference to sexual intercourse between a male and female. This sexual union of a male and female is the only way two people can become one flesh, even if they are not married to each other. One of the definitions for the Hebrew word "echad" means "same" (please see Genesis 11:1 & 6, NIV, NLT and AMP). Paul also indicated that marriage results in the man and the woman becoming the same person when he stated, "So ought men to love their wives as their own bodies. He that loveth his wife loveth himself" (Ephesians 5:28, KJV). "For no man ever yet hated his own flesh"

(Ephesians 5:29a, KJV). The Greek word for "own" means himself. Both "own" and "himself" come from the same Greek word, "heautou." When a man and a woman come together sexually, they again, become the same. They were once the same before God removed the rib from the man and made the woman. Upon a sexual union, they again become the same flesh. This is impossible with two men or two women. Two men and two women engaging in sex together can never become "the same." Oftentimes, people interpret this scripture to include emotional and spiritual oneness. However, Jesus wasn't referring to emotional or spiritual oneness. This principle was first introduced by God in Genesis and also recognized and taught to the Corinthian church by Paul. Paul indicates that any male who engages in a sexual act with a female, even with a prostitute, becomes one with her. "Don't you realize that your bodies are actually parts of Christ? Should a man take his body, which is part of Christ, and join it to a prostitute? Never! And don't you realize that if a man joins himself to a prostitute, he becomes one body with her? For the Scriptures say, 'The two are united into one.' But the person who is joined to the Lord is one spirit with him." (1 Corinthians. 6:15-17, NLT). Finally, an example of the language of the Old Testament that effected a marriage was, "...thou shalt go in unto her, and be her husband, and she shall by thy wife." (Deuteronomy 21:13, KJV)

JESUS COMMANDS - NO MARITAL CHANGES ARE ALLOWED

While the world is attempting to redefine marriage and loudly and vehemently advocating for this redefinition of marriage to include two men or two women, Jesus commanded that the arrangement for marriage is to forever remain to be between males and females. This exclusivity regarding marriage includes same sex marriages, "trans males" and "trans females." Trans man and trans woman is a misnomer, as it is impossible to trans into being a woman or a man. Changes made to one's body so that one can look like a male, or a female does not therefore make one a male or female. Only males and females' sexual unions are acceptable and blessed by God, with a very specific warning from Jesus against any human beings changing that marital and sexual arrangement. "Some Pharisees came and tried to trap him with this question: "Should a man be allowed to divorce his wife for just any reason?" "Haven't you read the Scriptures?" Jesus replied. "They record that from the beginning 'God made them male and female." "And he said, "'This explains why a man leaves his father and mother and is joined to his wife, and the two are united into one.' Since they are no longer two but one, let no one split apart what God has joined together." (Matthew 19:3-6, NLT). Jesus explicitly and prophetically commanded, "What therefore God hath joined together, let not man put asunder." (Matthew 19:6, KJV). In addition, Jesus did not leave this commandment ambiguous or up for interpretation. As He both reminds those who knew and informs all who would consider any alternative marital and sexual union, God joined together male and female. Jesus states, "So they are no longer two, but one flesh. Therefore what God has joined together, let no one separate." (Matthew 19:6, NIV)

As you will see with some of the translations, the definition of the Greek word used in this verse means to depart or separate. I like the term depart as a definition also, perhaps even more than I like separate. Depart is a simpler definition and I think is more consistent with Jesus's command and what Jesus had in mind. If Jesus was referring to two specific persons, separate would be just fine. However, on the other hand, if he has the sexes, male and female, in mind, and is actually warning against any departure from this arrangement, then depart would be, in my understanding, a better interpretation of the word and clearer to His audience. While the writers of the Bible may have written directly to God's people, indirectly, the Bible is God's Word to the world.

Some of you who are reading this book are aware that for decades, many Christians have even switched the word what, to who, or whom God hath joined together. However, this interpretation has opened the door for any two people, including two people of the same sex to claim that God has joined them together. It has also opened the door for people to subjectively claim another person's spouse as their own with the belief that the person whom they are claiming just married the wrong person. Generally speaking, God is not in the business of selecting mates for people. Conclusively, Jesus was not speaking of individual unions but sexes. That command and warning by Jesus is so much the more important and informative today in our current culture than ever before. What God hath joined together, let not man depart from it. No matter how many different types of relationship scenarios people come up with, it's not God's arrangement, nor are they ever blessed or recognized by God. All such unions, other than male and female, are illegitimate in the sight of God. Let the contemporary believer never forget, God joined together male and female, and Jesus warns that no man should ever change this divine arrangement.

THE FEMALE HAS A UNIQUE AND INDISPENSABLE ORIGIN AND PURPOSE

As indicated, being a male or female is not based on feelings, desires, preferences, likes, dislikes, acceptance, unacceptance, or any other arbitrary choice. The female was made. Female, as is male, is a biological creation. The female was created subsequent to the male being created, with different and distinct characteristics for the purpose of complementing, fulfilling the need of the male, and with the unique and indispensable ability to reproduce.

"Then the Lord God said, 'It is not good for the man to be alone. I will make a helper who is just right for him.' So the LORD God formed from the ground all the wild animals and all the birds of the sky. He brought them to the man to see what he would call them, and the man chose a name for each one. He gave names to all the livestock, all the birds of the sky, and all the wild animals. But still there was no helper just right for him. So the LORD God caused the man to fall into a deep sleep. While the man slept, the LORD God took out one of the man's ribs and closed up the opening. Then the Lord God made a woman from the rib, and he brought her to the man. 'At last!' the man exclaimed. 'This is bone from my bone, and flesh from my flesh! She will be called 'woman,' because she was taken from man.'" (Genesis 2:18-23, NLT).

The first thing that I want to point out is, the KJV appears to make "help meet" a single word and only lists the Greek word for "help." The Greek word for meet is not listed. However, other versions translate the verse with the Greek word "meet' in mind. The word is translated to suitable, complementary, complement, corresponding, like, suitable partner, or, just right by various translators. It appears that it is not easy to understand exactly what the word actually means. Yet, we have a pretty good idea. All the words the translators use, even though they may not have the best translation, appear to include some aspect of what God intended. It is clear that the woman was never meant to be exactly like the man. She is to be different. She is to be complementary. She is to be suitable. She is to be in front of him, in sight of him and opposite of him to fulfil the most intimate needs of both her and the man. So when God shares His purpose for creating the female, we learn what her relationship to the man should be. God stated that He would, in the KJV language, "make him an help meet for him." The Greek word meet, as listed above, means, "in front of, in sight of, or opposite to." All these phrases fit the position and purpose of the woman both biologically and sexually. Generally, things are made or otherwise invented with a purpose in mind. As such, they have certain features, characteristics, capabilities, abilities, and usability unique to that purpose. When God revealed His thoughts about the woman, the first thing He noted was that man was alone and that was not good. The second thing He noted is that He would not just create another person, but that He would create another person that would complement the man a person who would be opposite of him, yet complementary to him. Thus, everything about the woman, mentally, emotionally, psychologically, and physiologically, fits this purpose. When God indicated that man was alone, it was not simply that he didn't have anyone or anything else. It meant that he had no one that could meet certain needs and that he would create something or someone who could, and that something is a female. In this sense, male to male and female to female relationships are just as futile for meeting each other's need as an animal or any other creature God made and is equivalent to being alone. A female is the only creation of God that is made to fit the male's need.

"For the man is not of the woman; but the woman of the man." (1 Corinthians 11:8, KJV) Here, the Bible tells us that the man did not come out of the woman, but the woman came out of or out from the man. Paul is informing the Corinthians that the man did not originate from the woman, but the woman originated from the man. The Greek word "of" here is ek, which indicates out of, or out from within.

"Neither was the man created for the woman; but the woman for the man." (1 Corinthians 11:9, KJV). Here the Greek word is dia, which means through and indicates the channel of an act. The channel through which the woman came into being is through the man. Here, the emphasis is not necessarily or primarily of purpose, but again, Paul is driving down on origination, and reiterates how the woman came into being, that is, that the woman was created through the man. Paul is informing the Corinthian church, again, that the woman came into being through the man. So, in the abovementioned verses, Paul informs us that the woman came out of the man and through the man. Paul is not introducing a new doctrine but is just explaining Genesis 2:21-23 and virtually saying the same thing that God told Moses. The woman came out of man and into being through man.

Later on, Paul follows up with his message about the woman coming out of and through the man by seemingly suggesting, that just because she came out of and through the man, it doesn't mean that she is any less important. In fact, Paul seems to ultimately suggest that the woman would not exist but for the man, while later informing the man that the man would not continue without the woman. Paul states, "Nevertheless, neither is the man without the woman, neither the woman without the man, in the Lord. "The word without means, apart from, or separate. He continues and states, "For as the woman is of out of (ek) the man, even so, or in the same manner, is the man also by, which means through (the channel) the woman, but all things of (ek) God." See 1 Corinthians 11:11-12, KJV. At this point it is clear that Paul recognizes that without the continued cooperation and collaboration between the male and the female, the human race would come to an end.

Not only have we been informed of the origin and the channel through which the woman came, we are also informed of the indispensable necessity of both male and female. So, what do we have? Without God there would be no man, without man, there would be no woman, and without woman Adam would have been the last man. As any sane person can see, human beings would have been extinct nine hundred and thirty years from the time Adam was created, but for the woman, as Adam lived nine hundred and thirty years and he died. Homosexuality is a real existential threat to the continued growth and survival of mankind.

Not only is the woman indispensable for fulfilling the need of the man, but also for the continued existence of the human race. Every time two men or two women call for or unite in a sexual or "marital" relationship, they are directly and blatantly rebelling against the plan and purpose of God Himself regarding the unique purpose and continued survival and existence of humankind. It appears to be the worst kind of rebellion. Every believer ought to be clear about this and never compromise.

"Now the LORD God said, "It is not good (beneficial) for the man to be alone; I will make him a helper [one who balances him—a counterpart who is] suitable *and* complementary for him." (Genesis 2:18, AMP)

"The man gave names to all the livestock, to the birds of the sky, and to every wild animal; but for the man no helper was found as his complement." (Genesis 2:20, HCSB)

The female was not made for the purpose of joining with or fulfilling the sexual needs of another female. Females are not made with the ability to be joined sexually with another female. Neither males nor females are capable of fulfilling the need of another person of the same sex (or gender). Each was made with the physiological features to be complimentary and compatibly joined to the other. It is impossible for the female to become one with another female as the Bible explains would happen between a male and a female. The reason for this is that becoming one flesh is the result of the female, that was taken out of the male, being rejoined to the male. Thus, male joining to male sexually cannot become one flesh, nor can a female joining to another female become one flesh and therefore can never be married. Marriage is male and female consummating (becoming one through sexual intercourse) a legally authorized sexual union between a male and a female.

A critical point to be made and understood is that marriage is not primarily about becoming one in spirit, one in emotions, or one mentally, but becoming one flesh. While in a marriage people can develop a sense of oneness, the sexual union of a male and female is the only union that results in two human beings becoming one flesh. Paul tells us this by stating, "What? know ye not that he which is joined to an harlot is one body? for two, saith he, shall be one flesh." (1 Corinthians 6:16, KJV). From the beginning and throughout holy writ, marriage is described as a man joining or cleaving to his wife and becoming one flesh. Note, it does not simply say that they become one, but "one flesh." While all marriages result in the male and female becoming one flesh, all marriages do not result in the husband and wife becoming one in other ways, as that requires a different set of efforts and approaches. We need to get this right, because two men and two women are able to become one in mind, one in spirit, one emotionally, one in purpose, but never one physically or sexually.

Women are indispensable for the continued existence of the human race. Women are engineered for a unique purpose. It is utterly impossible for a man, regardless as to how he is changed, modified, transed, reengineered and what surgery is performed on him, to become a woman. A man and male is forever and always a man and male, and a woman and female is always and forever a woman and female until this mortal shall put on immortality and this corruptible shall have put on incorruption. Male and female is a fleshly and biological thing and it is much deeper than the external genitalia or any other external biological makeup or modification.

HOMOSEXUALITY IN THE OLD AND NEW TESTAMENT

If anyone wants to know what God thinks about homosexuality, the LGBTQ and transgenderism, they need look no further than Paul letters to the Gentile Church. What you will find is that the issues of fornication and sexual immorality, including homosexuality, are dealt with significantly more and graphically in both the Old Testament and the New Testament in what is known as the Christian church epistles of the New Testament in ways it is not dealt with in the gospels. It appears that in the Old Testament, fornication, including homosexuality, was primarily a practice of the heathen nations, more so than the Jews or Hebrews. References to the practice of homosexuality appear to indicate that other nations engaged in the practice of homosexuality and were responsible for introducing these forbidden practices to God's people. "Then the Lord said to Moses. Give the following instructions to the people of Israel. I am the Lord your God. So do not act like the people in Egypt, where you used to live, or like the people of Canaan, where I am taking you. You must not imitate their way of life. (Leviticus 18:1-3, NLT).

When Jesus spoke to John regarding His revelation to him, Jesus listed the introduction of sexual immorality to the nation of Israel as one of His concerns. He states, "Nevertheless, I have a few things against you: There are some among you who hold to the teaching of Balaam, who taught Balak to entice the Israelites to sin so that they ate food sacrificed to idols and committed sexual immorality." (Revelation 2:14, NIV).

There are a number of sexual sins that fall under fornication that Jesus did not mention but were identified in the Old Testament. See Leviticus 8:6-18 & 20:10-21. Please note that the following scriptures are noted for historical purposes and are exclusively listed for reviewing a list of forbidden sexual practices. The punishments listed for these sexual sins are categorically no longer in effect under our dispensation of grace and are categorically NOT supported or encouraged by Judeo-Christian believers today. An additional thing to note about the punishment of behavior that was considered sin in the Old Testament is that the punishment was indicative of the seriousness of how God viewed the sinful behavior. These legal mandates to stone people for certain sinful behavior were only in effect under the law and are not supported by any Christian or any person with a Biblical worldview today. Christ fulfilled the law, and these punishment mandates expired when He fulfilled the law. Today people who engage in these and other sins are expected to be treated with mercy, compassion, forgiveness, love, goodness, patience, tolerance, kindness, empathy, understanding, and sympathy. Furthermore, they are to be encouraged to place faith in Jesus Christ and receive forgiveness and deliverance.

For your review and consideration, I have listed the sexual relationships that were forbidden by God and thus considered to be wrong and sinful. Some of these sexual sins were deemed to be an abomination, which indicated that God viewed them as being morally disgusting or abhorrent. While Jesus never specifically mentioned most of the sins listed below, John the Baptist mentioned the sin of incest, and told Herod, "...it is not lawful for thee to have thy brother's wife." He was martyred by being decapitated. (Mark 6:18, KJV)

HOMOSEXUALITY IS CATEGORICALLY FORBIDDEN

LEVITICUS 18:22

"Do not have sexual relations with a man as one does with a woman; that is detestable. "(NIV)

"Do not practice homosexuality, having sex with another man as with a woman. It is a detestable sin." (NLT)

"Thou shalt not lie with mankind, as with womankind: it *is* abomination." (KJV)

LEVITICUS 20:13

"If a man has sexual relations with a man as one does with a woman, both of them have done what is detestable..." (NIV)

"If a man practices homosexuality, having sex with another man as with a woman, both men have committed a detestable act...." (NLT)

"If a man lies with a male as with a woman, both of them have committed an abomination..." (ESV)

"If a man lies with a man as with a woman, they have both committed an abomination...." (BSB)

"If a man also lie with mankind, as he lieth with a woman, both of them have committed an abomination..." (KJV)

"If a man lies with a male as he lies with a woman, both of them have committed an abomination." (NKJV)

FORBIDDEN SEXUAL RELATIONSHIPS IN THE OLD TESTAMENT

LEVITICUS 18:1-19, NLT

"Then the Lord said to Moses,

Give the following instructions to the people of Israel. I am the Lord your God.

So do not act like the people in Egypt, where you used to live, or like the people of Canaan, where I am taking you. You must not imitate their way of life.

You must obey all my regulations and be careful to obey my decrees, for I am the Lord your God. If you obey my decrees and my regulations, you will find life through them. I am the Lord You must never have sexual relations with a close relative, for I am the Lord. (Leviticus 18:1-6, NLT)

SEXUAL CONDUCT WITH RELATIVES, ALSO KNOWN BY OUR MODERN-DAY LAWS AS INCEST

MOTHER

"Do not violate your father by having sexual relations with your mother. She is your mother; you must not have sexual relations with her." (Leviticus 18:7)

STEPMOTHER

"Do not have sexual relations with any of your father's wives, for this would violate your father." (v. 8)

SISTER

"Do not have sexual relations with your sister or half-sister, whether she is your father's daughter or your mother's daughter, whether she was born into your household or someone else's." (v.9)

GRANDCHILD

"Do not have sexual relations with your granddaughter, whether she is your son's daughter or your daughter's daughter, for this would violate yourself." (v.10)

STEPSISTER

"Do not have sexual relations with your stepsister, the daughter of any of your father's wives, for she is your sister." (v. 11)

AUNT

"Do not have sexual relations with your father's sister, for she is your father's close relative. Do not have sexual relations with your mother's sister, for she is your mother's close relative. Do not violate your uncle, your father's brother, by having sexual relations with his wife, for she is your aunt." (v. 12-14)

IN-LAWS

"Do not have sexual relations with your daughter-in-law; she is your son's wife, so you must not have sexual relations with her. Do not have sexual relations with your brother's wife, for this would violate your brother." (v. 15-16)

OTHER SEXUAL BOUNDARIES

"Do not have sexual relations with both a woman and her daughter. And do not take her granddaughter, whether her son's daughter or her daughter's daughter, and have sexual relations with her. They are close relatives, and this would be a wicked act." (v. 17).

RESPECT

"While your wife is living, do not marry her sister and have sexual relations with her, for they would be rivals." (v. 18)

SANITARY SEXUAL ISSUES

"Do not have sexual relations with a woman during her period of menstrual impurity." (v. 19)

SINFUL AND FORBIDDEN SEXUAL ACTS IN THE OLD TESTAMENT

ADULTERY

Sex between one or more married person with anyone whom she he or she is not married to.

"Do not defile yourself by having sexual intercourse with your neighbor's wife." (Leviticus 18:20, NLT)

HOMOSEXUALITY

Sex between two men with the same biological sex at birth.

"Do not practice homosexuality, having sex with another man as with a woman. It is a detestable sin." (Leviticus 18: 22, NLT)

"If a man practices homosexuality, having sex with another man as with a woman, both men have committed a detestable act..." (Leviticus 20:13, NLT)

BESTIALITY

Sex between man and any animal.

"A man must not defile himself by having sex with an animal. And a woman must not offer herself to a male animal to have intercourse with it. This is a perverse act." (Leviticus 18:23, NLT)

INCEST

Leviticus 20:12

"If a man has sex with his daughter-in-law, both must be put to death. They have committed a perverse act and are guilty of a capital offense. (Lev 20:12, NLT)

Leviticus 20:17-21(NLT)

"If a man marries his sister, the daughter of either his father or his mother, and they have sexual relations, it is a shameful disgrace. They must be publicly cut off from the community. Since the man has violated his sister, he will be punished for his sin.

"If a man has sexual relations with a woman during her menstrual period, both of them must be cut off from the community, for together they have exposed the source of her blood flow.

"Do not have sexual relations with your aunt, whether your mother's sister or your father's sister. This would dishonor a close relative. Both parties are guilty and will be punished for their sin.

"If a man has sex with his uncle's wife, he has violated his uncle. Both the man and woman will be punished for their sin, and they will die childless.

"If a man marries his brother's wife, it is an act of impurity. He has violated his brother, and the guilty couple will remain childless. (Leviticus 20:17-21, NLT)

GENERAL ADMONITION AGAINST SEXUAL IMMORALITY

"Do not defile yourselves in any of these ways, for the people I am driving out before you have defiled themselves in all these ways. Because the entire land has become defiled, I am punishing the people who live there. I will cause the land to vomit them out. You must obey all my decrees and regulations. You must not commit any of these detestable sins. This applies both to native-born Israelites and to the foreigners living among you.

"All these detestable activities are practiced by the people of the land where I am taking you, and this is how the land has become defiled. So do not defile the land and give it a reason to vomit you out, as it will vomit out the people who live there now. Whoever commits any of these detestable sins will be cut off from the community of Israel.

So obey my instructions, and do not defile yourselves by committing any of these detestable practices that were committed by the people who lived in the land before you. I am the Lord your God." Leviticus 18:24-30, NLT

A REITERATION OF SEXUAL SINS ACCORDING TO THE BIBLE AND A BIBLICAL WORLDVIEW

While listing the forbidden sexual sins in the Bible and the biblical prohibitions listed above, there are laws in a number of states governing many of these sexual practices and most of these sexual practices, if not all, of them are yet forbidden today and thus criminalized. Nevertheless, though capital punishment for sexual sins is categorically forbidden by the church, there are certain sexual acts that carry very severe legal penalties. In addition to these legal penalties, there are also spiritual, moral, and biological consequences for sexual practices that are yet forbidden by God as listed in the Bible. In the New Testament, it is obvious that the practice of sexual immorality, including homosexuality, was not only present but prevalent among the gentile Christians as indicated in the books of Romans, Corinthians, and the church or churches overseen by Timothy. The issue is categorically addressed with these audiences and categorically listed as a member of the class of sexual sins.

HOMOSEXUALITY IS A SOCIAL CONSTRUCT AND THUS A HUMAN INVENTION

Jesus does not recognize homosexuality as being a creation of God. God created two distinct human beings that were identified as male and female. In addition, Jesus further explains God's sexual plan for the man and the woman. The man is to leave his father and mother and be joined to his wife and upon being joined, the man and the woman becomes one flesh. God joined men and women together and the man cleaves to his wife. God determines what should be joined together for cleaving purposes.

MALE AND FEMALE
NOT A SOCIAL CONSTRUCT OR A HUMAN INVENTION, BUT A DIVINE ARRANGEMENT

From a biblical worldview there were only two sexes created. These two sexes were identified as male and female. Male and female have a unique place in the human experience. Each was specifically created with unique and complementary qualities. Each was created with unique capabilities and abilities. Their unique build makes them uniquely suited for certain biological and physical roles that cannot be interchanged, reversed, or switched. Males and females were made to pair up and to complement each other. Those complemental qualities are designed to fulfill certain needs one of the other which cannot be met with any male to male or female to female relationship.

ACCEPTABLE ALTERNATIVE LIFESTYLE

In the last century, we have been introduced to concepts such as an "alternative lifestyle." In more recent years, homosexuality has been identified as an acceptable alternative lifestyle. However, a biblical worldview informs us that there is only one option by which males and females may fulfill their sexual needs or otherwise express themselves with another person sexually. The only other alternatives to male and female sex are, one, to remain as a single person, two, go further by becoming a eunuch and living a single life. The lifestyles related to sex are, to get married to a person of the opposite sex and live as married persons, remain single and live as a single person, or become a eunuch.

REMAINING SINGLE

Remaining single is practically the only alternative lifestyle to marriage between a male and a female. One can remain unmarried as a single person and continue to deal with all the challenges related to being a single person. In this case sexual desire, sexual challenges, biological changes including the effect of the testosterone and the estrogen and other hormone are highly likely to cause one who is healthy and has a healthy sex drive, to feel sexual and in some cases respond sexually, even if it is inadvertently or unintentionally. On the other hand, castration addresses this issue and the person who is castrated.

BORN OR BECOMING A EUNUCH

The other two alternate lifestyle indicated in the Bible is to become a eunuch or to remain celibate. A eunuch is a male who has been castrated. One notable reason why men get castrated today is for medical reasons and not necessarily for sexual reasons, especially in North America. Jesus stated, regarding eunuchs, "For there are eunuchs who were born that way, and there are eunuchs who have been made eunuchs by others—and there are those who choose to live like eunuchs for the sake of the kingdom of heaven. The one who can accept this should accept it." (Matthew 19:12, NIV) Though becoming a eunuch is said to reduce sexual desire and urges, it does not totally remove all urges and sexual desire based on testosterone levels. However, they are unable to have children.

REMAINING CELIBATE

Regarding remaining celibate is also an acceptable alternative lifestyle to marriage as it relates to male and female and sexual choices. Men and women in different religions choose to remain celibate for ministry reasons. Paul stated the following regarding living a life of celibacy, "I want you to be free from the concerns of this life. An unmarried man can spend his time doing the Lord's work and thinking how to please him. But a married man has to think about his earthly responsibilities and how to please his wife. His interests are divided. In the same way, a woman who is no longer married or has never been married can be devoted to the Lord and holy in body and in spirit. But a married woman has to think about her earthly responsibilities and how to please her husband. I am saying this for your benefit, not to place restrictions on you. I want you to do whatever will help you serve the Lord best, with as few distractions as possible." (1 Corinthians 7:32-35, NLT). Neither of these choices denies their biological sex or attempts to identify as a sex other than their biological sex.

HOMOSEXUALITY:
THE ROOT CAUSE

The root cause of homosexuality is not genetic in the sense that people claim. The only thing that comes close to homosexuality having a genetic component is sin. Sin impacts the genes and all related biological and physiological processes. All of creation, including human beings, are infected with sin. Sin permeates and affects us biopsychosocially and spiritually. Homosexuality is an act of lasciviousness which is described as unbridled lust, excess, licentiousness, wantonness, outrageousness, shamelessness, and insolence. It's outside of the realm of normality and moral decency. While there are many that are engaging in and promoting this immoral lifestyle, that does not make it right. The practice of homosexuality is also an act of depravity. At the end of the day, the root cause is sin.

NEW TESTAMENT EXPLANATION OF THE CAUSE AND DEVELOPMENT OF HOMOSEXUALITY

Homosexuality is a social construct and unnatural, therefore the spread of homosexual behavior and relationships from one generation to another is dependent on interacting social networks such as peers, family members, other social influences, propaganda, social learning, modeling, proselytizing and other ways behavior is taught and caught.

The more homosexuals, the more LGBTQ, and transgender people we have, the more we will have, not by birth but by propaganda. However, in order for this to happen, there has to be a continuation of the major causes of its growth, which are suppression of the truth and rejection of the truth.

SUPPRESSION OF THE TRUTH

"But God shows his anger from heaven against all sinful, wicked people who suppress the truth by their wickedness." (Romans 1:18, NLT)

REJECTION OF THE TRUTH

"They know the truth about God because he has made it obvious to them. For ever since the world was created, people have seen the earth and sky. Through everything God made, they can clearly see his invisible qualities—his eternal power and divine nature. So they have no excuse for not knowing God. Yes, they knew God, but they wouldn't worship him as God or even give him thanks. And they began to think up foolish ideas of what God was like. As a result, their minds became dark and confused. Claiming to be wise, they instead became utter fools. And instead of worshiping the glorious, ever-living God, they worshiped idols made to look like mere people and birds and animals and reptiles. So God abandoned them to do whatever shameful things their hearts desired. As a result, they did vile and degrading things with each other's bodies. They traded the truth about God for a lie. So they worshiped and served the things God created instead of the Creator himself, who is worthy of eternal praise! Amen. That is why God abandoned them to their shameful desires. Even the women turned against the natural way to have sex and instead indulged in sex with each other. And the men, instead of having normal sexual relations with women, burned with lust for each other. Men did shameful things with other men, and as a result of this sin, they suffered within themselves the penalty they deserved. Since they thought it foolish to acknowledge God, he abandoned them to their foolish thinking and let them do things that should never be done." (Romans 1:19-28, NLT)

Homosexual behavior is a result of rebellion against God and the revelation of the truth of God and is manifested by the following acts:

1. Suppression of the truth
2. Rejection of the truth
3. A failure to glorify or honor God
4. A failure to give God thanks
5. Becoming futile in their thinking
6. Darkened hearts
7. Claiming to be wise (pride and arrogance)
8. Becoming a fool, or deceived
9. Reducing God to images of mortal men, birds, animals, and reptiles

THE CONSEQUENCES OF THE REJECTION AND SUPPRESSION OF THE TRUTH

1. Given over to sinful desires
2. Given over to sexual impurity
3. Engages in the Degrading of each other's body
4. Exchanged the truth of God for a lie
5. Given over to shameful lusts
6. Changed the natural sexual relationship of women for unnatural relationships
7. Men abandoned the natural relationship of men with women
8. Men became inflamed by their lust
9. Men engaged in shameful acts with each other

HOMOSEXUALITY IS A MUTABLE CHARACTERISTIC

Those who deny this scientific fact only deny it when the issue is a change from being a homosexual to being a heterosexual. Yet changing from being heterosexual to homosexual is accepted and applauded. The justification for this claim is that one who has homosexual interest and tendencies has not changed but they have always had these feelings and are simply coming out or finally accepting what they have always known to be true of themselves.

This truth is known by the religious community and is also known by the scientific community. Any serious scientist could easily document the dynamic and immutable condition of homosexuality by way of a longitudinal study. Even without this longitudinal study there are numerous reports of people who previously identified as homosexual and are now living a very normal heterosexual life with a spouse of the opposite sex and children. Here's a record reporting that there are people who were once homosexuals and after becoming a believer and receiving the Holy Spirit, they were changed and were no longer homosexuals, or engaging in the sinful behaviors that they used to engage in.

"Don't you realize that those who do wrong will not inherit the Kingdom of God? Don't fool yourselves. Those who indulge in sexual sin, or who worship idols, or commit adultery, or are male prostitutes, or practice homosexuality, or are thieves, or greedy people, or drunkards, or are abusive, or cheat people— none of these will inherit the Kingdom of God. Some of you were once like that. But you were cleansed; you were made holy; you were made right with God by calling on the name of the Lord Jesus Christ and by the Spirit of our God." (1 Corinthian 6:9-11, NLT). Here, we have a clear report that homosexuals can change and have changed.

Struggling with a behavior or a lifestyle once a person has

overcome it or come out of a particular lifestyle is not indicative of the immutability of the lifestyle or behavior, but of the
powerful impact that such a lifestyle has on human nature,
whether this be drugs, alcohol, gambling, greed, being a thief,
or sexual immorality.

IMMUTABLE CONDITIONS ARE NOT SINFUL

All sinful behaviors and conditions condemned by God are mutable. Human beings have the ability to change any mutable conditions. Immutable conditions are unchangeable. God does not condemn immutable attributes. While there are immutable conditions that are caused by sin, immutable conditions are never condemned in scripture. God only condemns those behaviors that are sinful and mutable. God recognizes that race and other things are immutable. "Can an Ethiopian change the color of his skin? Can a leopard take away its spots?" (Jeremiah 13:23, NLT) These are rhetorical questions regarding immutable characteristics such as the color of a person's skin and the leopard having spots, with the answer being no. This is unlike the ability of a person to change their mutable sexual behavior, as with all sexual immorality, including homosexuality.

A NEW TESTAMENT
CATEGORIZATION OF
HOMOSEXUALITY

Homosexuality is no more simply a genetic or immutable condition than any other sexual sin or any other sinful behavior. Homosexuality is categorized as sinful and unrighteous and listed with many other sins.

"Don't you realize that those who do wrong will not inherit the Kingdom of God? Don't fool yourselves. Those who indulge in sexual sin, or who worship idols, or commit adultery, or are male prostitutes, or practice homosexuality..." (1 Corinthians 6:9, NLT)

"The law is for people who are sexually immoral, or who practice homosexuality, or are slave traders, liars, promise breakers, or who do anything else that contradicts the wholesome teaching." (1 Timothy 1:10, NLT)

HOMOSEXUALITY IS
SEXUAL IMMORALITY

It is clear, based on the scriptures listed above, that homosexuality is compared to other sexual sins including adultery, whoremongering, prostitution, bestiality, child sex, group sex, and polygamy, and is sexually immoral.

HOMOSEXUALITY: PREVENTS ENTRANCE INTO THE KINGDOM OF GOD

According to the Bible, immutable traits such as race or color of skin do not prevent anyone from entering into the kingdom of God. There is not a single verse of scripture that suggests that one cannot enter the kingdom of God or otherwise be saved because of the color of their skin or any other immutable condition. Only those choices and behaviors that men choose to engage in, voluntarily, prevent people from entering the kingdom of God. Being born again, also referred to as birth from above and regeneration, are indispensable requirements for entering the kingdom of God. And as a believer and member of the kingdom of God, we are expected to live a life of obedience to God by endeavoring to comply with the commands of scripture. Our lives are to be ordered by principles of godliness, righteousness, and sanctification. We are also expected to experience a dynamic spiritual change, access into power of God and spiritual gifts. Regeneration is the ultimate cure to homosexuality. There is a life and death difference between being a church member, having powerful emotional experiences, feeling accepted and loved by God, participating in church worship and serving in ministry, and actually being saved and born again. One can have great emotional experiences for many reasons and do all the things listed above and yet be neither saved nor born again. A person will not continue to have homosexual desires and practice homosexuality without being convicted by the Holy Spirit, if that person has experienced regeneration.

"Don't you realize that those who do wrong will not inherit the Kingdom of God? (1 Corinthians 6:9, NLT). "Those who belong to Christ Jesus have nailed the passions and desires of their sinful nature to his cross and crucified them there." (Galatians 5:24, NLT). "Jesus replied, 'I tell you the truth, unless you are born again, you cannot see the Kingdom of God.'" "Jesus replied,

'I assure you, no one can enter the Kingdom of God without being born of water and the Spirit." (John 3:3 & 5)

I know that there are many in the homosexual community who claim to be Christians. This is no truer than anyone else who claims to be a Christian and refuses to comply with the Word of God. One who practices homosexuality, and other acts of sexual immorality, will never be able to experience God's best in this life. Paul tells us that the characteristics of the kingdom of God are "righteousness, and peace, and joy in the Holy Ghost." (Romans 14:17, KJV) He also adds that it's "not in word, but in power." (1 Corinthians 4:20) One who is a member of the Kingdom of God is given the will and the ability to live a godly (righteous) life and have the power of God working in and through them to enable them to live according to God's Word. A true characteristic of being a believer, especially a born-again believer, is not perfection, but a desire and an effort to live like the Savior wants us to live.

LIVING BY A HIGHER STANDARD

Christians are expected to live by a high moral standard and to be guided by Christian principles.

Human beings have to be guided by standards of morality, decency, laws, principles, values, self-control, and such. They are not beings that are merely subject to or guided by instinct. Neither are they thoughtless creatures who live out their desires without regard to these standards of living. Instinct is defined as 1. an innate, species-specific biological force that impels an organism to do something, particularly to perform a certain act or respond in a certain manner to specific stimuli.an innate, typically fixed pattern of behavior in animals in response to certain stimuli. "Birds have an instinct to build nests." Retrieved from https://www.google.com/search?q=instinct+meaning

Human beings don't live their lives by instinct. We are not guided by a philosophy that states, "If it feels good, do it."

We control our urges and desires, our urges and desires do not control us. Paul states,

"You say, 'I am allowed to do anything'—but not everything is good for you. And even though 'I am allowed to do anything,' I must not become a slave to anything. You say, 'Food was made for the stomach, and the stomach for food.' (This is true, though someday God will do away with both of them.) But you can't say that our bodies were made for sexual immorality. They were made for the Lord, and the Lord cares about our bodies. And God will raise us from the dead by his power, just as he raised our Lord from the dead." (1 Corinthians 6:12-14, NLT)

Feelings can be a poor indicator of right and wrong. It can feel so right but be so wrong.

Nor is the rightness of any matter based solely on how many people think it's right or wrong. Right and wrong is determined by God, and not by the vote of the populace.

THE STORY OF AN ACTUAL HOMOSEXUALITY INCIDENT IN THE BIBLE

GENESIS 19:1-16
NEW INTERNATIONAL VERSION

"The two angels arrived at Sodom in the evening, and Lot was sitting in the gateway of the city. When he saw them, he got up to meet them and bowed down with his face to the ground. 'My lords,' he said, 'please turn aside to your servant's house. You can wash your feet and spend the night and then go on your way early in the morning.'

'No,' they answered, 'we will spend the night in the square.'

"But he insisted so strongly that they did go with him and entered his house. He prepared a meal for them, baking bread without yeast, and they ate. Before they had gone to bed, all the men from every part of the city of Sodom—both young and old—surrounded the house. They called to Lot, 'Where are the men who came to you tonight? Bring them out to us so that we can have sex with them.'

Lot went outside to meet them and shut the door behind him and said, 'No, my friends. Don't do this wicked thing. Look, I have two daughters who have never slept with a man. Let me bring them out to you, and you can do what you like with them. But don't do anything to these men, for they have come under the protection of my roof.'"

'Get out of our way,' they replied. 'This fellow came here as a foreigner, and now he wants to play the judge! We'll treat you worse than them.' They kept bringing pressure on Lot and moved forward to break down the door.

But the men inside reached out and pulled Lot back into the house and shut the door. Then they struck the men who were at the door of the house, young and old, with blindness so that they could not find the door.

The two men said to Lot, 'Do you have anyone else here— sons-in-law, sons or daughters, or anyone else in the city who belongs to you? Get them out of here, because we are going to destroy this place. The outcry to the Lord against its people is so great that he has sent us to destroy it.'

So Lot went out and spoke to his sons-in-law, who were pledged to marry his daughters. He said, 'Hurry and get out of this place, because the Lord is about to destroy the city!' But his sons-in-law thought he was joking.

With the coming of dawn, the angels urged Lot, saying, 'Hurry! Take your wife and your two daughters who are here, or you will be swept away when the city is punished.'

When he hesitated, the men grasped his hand and the hands of his wife and of his two daughters and led them safely out of the city, for the Lord was merciful to them. As soon as they had brought them out, one of them said, 'Flee for your lives! Don't look back, and don't stop anywhere in the plain! Flee to the mountains or you will be swept away!'"

This actual story of a homosexual incident in the Bible demonstrates a group of people who were aggressive, disrespect-ful of the rights and opinions of others, violent, driven by their sexuality, insistent on doing what they wanted to do, forcing themselves on others and violating their rights and their space. These same behaviors are consistent with and are characteristic of the LGBTQ and Transgender movement of today.

THE RECORD OF THE DESTRUCTION OF SODOM AND GOMORRAH

"At dawn the next morning the angels became insistent. 'Hurry,' they said to Lot. 'Take your wife and your two daughters who are here. Get out right now, or you will be swept away in the destruction of the city!' When Lot still hesitated, the angels seized his hand and the hands of his wife and two daughters and rushed them to safety outside the city, for the LORD was merciful. When they were safely out of the city, one of the angels ordered, 'Run for your lives! And don't look back or stop anywhere in the valley! Escape to the mountains, or you will be swept away!'" (Genesis 19:15-17, NLT)

"By the time Lot reached Zoar, the sun had risen over the land. Then the Lord rained down burning sulfur on Sodom and Gomorrah—from the Lord out of the heavens. Thus he overthrew those cities and the entire plain, destroying all those living in the cities—and also the vegetation in the land. But Lot's wife looked back, and she became a pillar of salt. Early the next morning Abraham got up and returned to the place where he had stood before the Lord. He looked down toward Sodom and Gomorrah, toward all the land of the plain, and he saw dense smoke rising from the land, like smoke from a furnace. So when God destroyed the cities of the plain, he remembered Abraham, and he brought Lot out of the catastrophe that overthrew the cities where Lot had lived." (Genesis 19:23-29 NIV)

"It was the same in the days of Lot. People were eating and drinking, buying and selling, planting and building. But the day Lot left Sodom, fire and sulfur rained down from heaven and destroyed them all." (Luke 17:28-29, NIV)

"if he condemned the cities of Sodom and Gomorrah by burning them to ashes, and made them an example of what is going to happen to the ungodly; and if he rescued Lot, a righteous man, who was distressed by the depraved conduct of the lawless (for that righteous man, living among them day after day, was tormented in his righteous soul by the lawless deeds he saw and heard)." (2 Peter 2:6-8, NIV)

HOMOSEXUALITY WAS CLEARLY ONE OF THE REASONS SODOM AND GOMORRAH WAS DESTROYED

"'As surely as I live, declares the Sovereign LORD, your sister Sodom and her daughters never did what you and your daughters have done. Now this was the sin of your sister Sodom: She and her daughters were arrogant, overfed and unconcerned; they did not help the poor and needy. They were haughty and did detestable things before me. Therefore I did away with them as you have seen.'" (Ezekiel 16:48-50, NIV)

"And don't forget Sodom and Gomorrah and their neighboring towns, which were filled with immorality and every kind of sexual perversion. Those cities were destroyed by fire and serve as a warning of the eternal fire of God's judgment." Jude 1:7, NLT)

HOMOSEXUALITY IS SEXUAL IMMORALITY AND IS INCLUDED WITHIN THE LIST OF SEXUAL SINS AND OTHER SINS

1 CORINTHIANS 6:9-11

NIV

"Or do you not know that wrongdoers will not inherit the kingdom of God? Do not be deceived: Neither the sexually immoral nor idolaters nor adulterers nor men who have sex with men, nor thieves nor the greedy nor drunkards nor slanderers nor swindlers will inherit the kingdom of God. And that is what some of you were. But you were washed, you were sanctified, you were justified in the name of the Lord Jesus Christ and by the Spirit of our God."

NLT

"Don't you realize that those who do wrong will not inherit the Kingdom of God? Don't fool yourselves. Those who indulge in sexual sin, or who worship idols, or commit adultery, or are male prostitutes, or practice homosexuality, or are thieves, or greedy people, or drunkards, or are abusive, or cheat people— none of these will inherit the Kingdom of God. Some of you were once like that. But you were cleansed; you were made holy; you were made right with God by calling on the name of the Lord Jesus Christ and by the Spirit of our God."

KJV

"Know ye not that the unrighteous shall not inherit the kingdom of God? Be not deceived: neither fornicators, nor idolaters, nor adulterers, nor effeminate, nor abusers of themselves with mankind, Nor thieves, nor covetous, nor drunkards, nor revilers, nor extortioners, shall inherit the kingdom of God. And such were some of you: but ye are washed, but ye are sanctified, but ye are justified in the name of the Lord Jesus, and by the Spirit of our God."

I TIMOTHY 1:8-10
NIV

"We know that the law is good if one uses it properly. We also know that the law is made not for the righteous but for lawbreakers and rebels, the ungodly and sinful, the unholy and irreligious, for those who kill their fathers or mothers, for murderers, for the sexually immoral, for those practicing homosexuality, for slave traders and liars and perjurers—and for whatever else is contrary to the sound doctrine that conforms to the gospel concerning the glory of the blessed God, which he entrusted to me."

NLT

We know that the law is good when used correctly. For the law was not intended for people who do what is right. It is for people who are lawless and rebellious, who are ungodly and sinful, who consider nothing sacred and defile what is holy, who kill their father or mother or commit other murders. The law is for people who are sexually immoral, or who practice homosexuality, or are slave traders, liars, promise breakers, or who do anything else that contradicts the wholesome teaching that comes from the glorious Good News entrusted to me by our blessed God.

THE ORIGIN OF
HOMOSEXUALITY EXPLAINED

The practice of homosexuality is described and explained in the following verses.

"The wrath of God is being revealed from heaven against all the godlessness and wickedness of people, who suppress the truth by their wickedness, Since what may be known about God is plain to them, because God has made it plain to them. For since the creation of the world God's invisible qualities—his eternal power and divine nature—have been clearly seen, being understood from what has been made, so that people are without excuse."

"For although they knew God, they neither glorified him as God nor gave thanks to him, but their thinking became futile and their foolish hearts were darkened. Although they claimed to be wise, they became fools and exchanged the glory of the immortal God for images made to look like a mortal human being and birds and animals and reptiles. "Therefore God gave them over in the sinful desires of their hearts to sexual impurity for the degrading of their bodies with one another. They exchanged the truth about God for a lie, and worshiped and served created things rather than the Creator—who is forever praised. Amen."

"Because of this, God gave them over to shameful lusts. Even their women exchanged natural sexual relations for unnatural ones. In the same way the men also abandoned natural relations with women and were inflamed with lust for one another. Men committed shameful acts with other men, and received in themselves the due penalty for their error."

"Furthermore, just as they did not think it worthwhile to retain the knowledge of God, so God gave them over to a depraved mind, so that they do what ought not to be done. They have become filled with every kind of wickedness, evil, greed and depravity. They are full of envy, murder, strife, deceit and malice. They are gossips, slanderers, God-haters, insolent, arrogant and boastful; they invent ways of doing evil; they disobey their parents; they have no understanding, no fidelity, no love, no mercy." Romans 1:18-31, NIV)

40 IRREFUTABLE REASONS WHY HOMOSEXUALITY AND TRANS- GENDERISM IS DETRIMENTAL TO INDIVIDUALS, AMERICA, AND THE WORLD

1. The homosexuals, lesbians, transgenders, and other members of the LGBTQ+ communities' sexual practices are in direct and unequivocal opposition to God's ideas for human sexual practice and expression.

   "Thou shalt not lie with mankind, as with womankind: it is abomination. (Leviticus 18:22, KJV)

   "Do not practice homosexuality, having sex with another man as with a woman. It is a detestable sin." (Leviticus 18:22, NLT)

   "If a man also lie with mankind, as he lieth with a woman, both of them have committed an abomination..." (Leviticus 20:13, KJV)

   "If a man practices homosexuality, having sex with another man as with a woman, both men have committed a detestable act..." (Leviticus 20:13, NLT)

2. The paring of homosexuals, lesbians, transgender, and other members of the LBBTQ+ communities for sexual relationships are in direct and unequivocal opposition to God's purpose for the creation of the female and his goal of providing the man with a person who would be different from him, opposite of him, complementary to him and suitable for him.

"The LORD God said, "It is not good for the man to be alone. I will make a helper suitable for him." (Genesis 2:18, NIV).

"So, the man gave names to all the livestock, the birds in the sky and all the wild animals. But for Adam no suitable helper was found." (Genesis 2:20, NIV)

"So, the LORD God caused the man to fall into a deep sleep; and while he was sleeping, he took one of the man's ribs and then closed up the place with flesh." (Genesis 2:21, NIV).

"Then the LORD God made a woman from the rib he had taken out of the man, and he brought her to the man." (Genesis 2:22, NIV)

3. The joining together of homosexuals, lesbians, transgender, and other members of the LGBTQ+ communities for sexual practices are in direct and unequivocal opposition to human nature and is therefore unnatural and contrary to the inherent features and characteristic of normal and natural human sexual attractions, affections, desire, and practice.

"For this cause God gave them up unto vile affections: for even their women did change the natural use into that which is against nature:" (Romans 1:26, KJV)

"That is why God abandoned them to their shameful desires. Even the women turned against the natural way to have sex and instead indulged in sex with each other." (Romans 1:26, NLT)

"And likewise also the men, leaving the natural use of the woman, burned in their lust one toward another; men with men working that which is unseemly, and receiving in themselves that recompence of their error which was meet." (Romans 1:27, KJV) "And the men, instead of having normal sexual relations with women, burned with lust for each other. Men did shameful things with other men, and as a result of this sin, they suffered within themselves the penalty they deserved." (Romans 1:27, NLT).

"And even as they did not like to retain God in *their* knowledge, God gave them over to a reprobate mind, to do those things which are not convenient;" Romans 1:28, KJV)

"Since they thought it foolish to acknowledge God, he abandoned them to their foolish thinking and let them do things that should never be done." (Romans 1:28, NLT)

4. The sexual practices and promotion of homosexual, lesbians, transgenders, and other members of the LGBTQ+ communities are a direct contravention of God's command to be fruitful and multiply.

"And God blessed them, and God said unto them, Be fruitful, and multiply, and replenish the earth, and subdue it: and have dominion over the fish of the sea, and over the fowl of the air, and over every living thing that moveth upon the earth." (Gen 1:28, KJV)

"Then God blessed them and said, 'Be fruitful and multiply. Fill the earth and govern it. Reign over the fish in the sea, the birds in the sky, and all the animals that scurry along the ground." (Genesis 1:28, NLT)

"And God blessed Noah and his sons, and said unto them, Be fruitful, and multiply, and replenish the earth.'" (Genesis 9:1, KJV)

"Then God blessed Noah and his sons and told them, '"Be fruitful and multiply. Fill the earth.'" (Genesis 9:1, NLT)

"And you, be ye fruitful, and multiply; bring forth abundantly in the earth, and multiply therein." (Genesis 9:7, KJV)

"Now be fruitful and multiply, and repopulate the earth." (Genesis 9:7, NLT)

5. Only biological males and biological females can become one flesh.

"And the LORD God caused a deep sleep to fall upon Adam, and he slept: and He took one of his ribs, and closed up the flesh in its place. Then the rib which the LORD God had taken from man, He made into a woman, and He brought her to the man. And Adam said: 'This is now bone of my bones, And flesh of my flesh; She shall be called Woman, Because she was taken out of Man.' Therefore a man shall leave his father and mother and be joined to his wife, and they shall become one flesh." (Genesis 2:21-24, KJV)

"And he answered, and said to them, 'Have you not read that He who made them at the beginning "made them male and female," and said, "For this reason a man shall leave his father and mother and be joined to his wife, and the two shall become one flesh"? So then, they are no longer two but one flesh. Therefore what God has joined together, let not man separate.'" (Matthew 19:4-6).

In both the Old and New Testament, becoming one flesh, also indicated as marriage, is an exclusive ability of male and female unions. In both passages of scripture, we are given the reason for this exclusive relationship of the male and female becoming one flesh, that is "because" the woman was taken out of man. It's not simply two people coming together for sex but due to the design and origin of the female.

6. There are obvious distinctions between the biological characteristics of a male and a female.

   These differences are based on empirical evidence and have been accepted by both the scientific and religious community. There is a created difference between male and female, also referred to as man and woman. They are different to their very genotype or genetic constitution. However, this generation seeks to reject the idea of male and female and their differences. The distinctions between male and female are so obvious that one must be disingenuous or delusional to deny them.

7. Many homosexuals, lesbians, transgenders, and members of the LGBTQ+ communities acknowledge God, are religious, and many claim to be Christians. As such, they seek to have their "marriages" sanctioned and blessed by God. However, only biological male and female sexual unions are sanctioned and blessed by God. Any other sexual union is neither accepted by nor blessed by God.

"So God created human beings in his own image. In the image of God He created them; male and female he created them." (Genesis 1:27, NLT)

"Then God blessed them and said, 'Be fruitful and multiply.'" (Genesis 1:28a. NLT)

"Since they are no longer two but one, let no one split apart what God has joined together." (Matthew 19:6, NLT) "What" refers to male and female. Jesus explicitly commands that no one should depart from the type of marital arrangement that He has set up, which is male and female becoming one flesh. The King James Version states, "...What therefore God hath joined together, let not man put asunder." (Matthew 19:6, KJV)

8. Not only are same sex unions, even if they are legal, a contravention of God's commandment to be fruitful and multiply, but it is also categorically impossible for same sex unions to carry out God's command to be fruitful and to multiply.

"Then God blessed Noah and his sons and told them, 'Be fruitful and multiply. Fill the earth.'" (Genesis 9:1, NLT) (See also Genesis 1:28, NLT).

9. Since God wanted human beings to continue their existence on earth and for the earth to be replenished with what He had created, male and female pairing was ordered by God for the purpose of keeping humanity and all other living creatures alive during and after the flood.

"And of every living thing of all flesh, two of every sort shalt thou bring into the ark, to keep them alive with thee; they shall be male and female." (Genesis 6:19, KJV)

"Bring a pair of every kind of animal – a male and a female – into the boat with you to keep them alive during the flood." (Genesis 6:19, NLT).

"So Noah did everything as the LORD commanded him. Noah was 600 years old when the flood covered the earth. He went on board the boat to escape the flood—he and his wife and his sons and their wives." (Genesis 7:5-7, NLT)

10. Male and female sexual unions always have, and always will be indispensable for the continuity of life as we know it.

11. No homosexual, lesbian, transgender, sexual union of persons of the same biological sex, or any other sexual union of persons of the same biological sex can cause the other person of the same biological sex to conceive or bring forth another human being.

"For the first man didn't come from woman, but the first woman came from man." (1 Corinthians, 11:8, NLT) Here, Paul explicitly tells the Gentile Christians that the first man didn't come out of the woman, but the first woman came out of the man. (See Genesis 2:21-24 above.)

"And man was not made for woman, but woman for man." (1 Corinthians 11:9, NLT) The scripture would be better translated as follows: "And man was not made or created through the woman, but the woman was made or created through the man." In this verse, the Greed word for "for" is "dia" and means through. Paul tells the church that the first man didn't come through the woman, but on the other hand the first woman came through the man.

Paul adds, "Nevertheless, in the Lord woman is not independent of man, nor is man independent of the woman." (1 Corinthians 11:11, NIV) The meaning of this scripture, in context, is there would be no woman without the first man, Adam, as the first woman came out from the first man and there are no additional men other than Adam without the woman because every man, other than Adam is brought forth through the woman.

12. The teachings and sexual practices of the homosexual, lesbian, transgender, and members of the LGBTQ+ communities are among the biggest existential threats to God's conception of the nuclear parent family consisting of a male and female in the role of father and mother.

"Honor thy father and thy mother: that thy days may be long upon the land which the LORD thy God giveth thee." (Exodus 20:12, KJV) Mothers are females and are incapable of being fathers as fathers are males and incapable of being mothers in virtually every way imageable. A mother, who is a female, has unique characteristic as does a father, who is a male. Even though it's impossible to completely mimic the opposite sex. In a homosexual or lesbian relationship, where both people are of the same sex, and with at least one of the same sex couples seeking to copy or mimic the opposite sex. Children need the natural and genuine feminine virtues of a biological woman for a mother and the natural and genuine masculinity of a biological man for a father; no imitations will do. While these make-believe women and make-believe men are fulfilling their fantasies, the children who are being raised by same sex couples are being robbed of the real experiences and benefits of motherhood and fatherhood. Male to male and female to female sexual unions only serve to fulfill the personal and selfish sexual passions, desires and interests of those individuals while depriving the children whom they have adopted or are otherwise raising in such a relationship, of the benefit of two parents or caregivers of the opposite sex who can provide unique care.

13. In particular, the sexual practices of homosexuality, lesbianism, transgenderism, and members of the LGBTQ communities are among the biggest threats to the healthy development, growth, and survival of the African American race.

First, for those who would say that I am homophobic, or this book is homophobic, they are so far from the truth if they are alleging that my concerns and fears are irrational, or personal, or if they are alleging that there is any unfair targeting or discrimination against the members of this community. The fear that I have is real and based on empirical evidence. If you want to say that I am "fearful," okay. However, my fears are not irrational, but very informed. It's a care and concern-based fear. I am fearful of the impact that homosexuality, lesbianism, transgenderism, and other same sex practices of other members of the LGBTQ+ have and will continue to have on individuals, communities, our nation, and the world. I am fearful of the ubiquitous propagandizing, proselytizing, and the forced acceptance of this lifestyle upon parents, caregivers, minor children, work colleagues, Christians, and the general population. I am fearful of the efforts of this community to infiltrate our preschools, elementary schools, high schools and our libraries with pornographic literature and behavior. I am fearful of the efforts of members of this community to indoctrinate and proselytize the most vulnerable. I am fearful of the short and long-term negative impact of the efforts, by members of this community and those who support their sexual practices, to provide body altering medication and surgeries that will irreparably harm children. But I am not "homophobic" as the term is used towards those who simply disagree with this lifestyle or dare to speak the truth. More importantly, it's not simply what I believe, but what God says, commands and expects.

I mention my concerns regarding the impact of the behaviors that members of the homosexual, lesbian, transgender, and LGBTQ+ communities will have on African Americans because African Americans are already reported to suffer at a greater percentage from abortion, medically related diseases and issues, disproportionate crime victimhood, criminal justice contacts and incarceration, maleducation and ineducation, and substance use disorders (drug and alcohol addiction).

Article by Right to Life Michigan, "Black Abortions By The Numbers. "More than 20 million Black babies have been aborted since the 1973 Roe v. Wade U.S. Supreme Court decision legalized abortion in our country. Non-Hispanic Black women have a significantly higher abortion rate (24.4 per 1000 women of reproductive age) than that of Non-Hispanic Whites (6.2) and Hispanics (11.4). 39.2% of all reported abortions in the U.S. in 2020 were performed on Black women, however, only about 12.4% of the total population is Black. African Americans are no longer the nation's largest minority group... For every 1,000 live births, non-Hispanic Black women had 426 abortions. Retrieved from https://rtl.org/multicultural-outreach/ black-abortion-statistics/

While this population has already suffered disproportionately from abortion, if you add homosexuality, lesbianism, transgenderism and the LGBTQ+ agenda and practices that include men pairing with men, male children having their genitals amputated and altered, women having their genitals replaced with male genitals, hormone treatments to alter the natural growth and development of the male and the female bodies, and those children being reared, propagandized, and proselytized by the LGBTQ+ communities, and other public and private institutions, the impact on African American children, families, and communities will be devastating. African Americans, though they are a smaller percentage of the population, are projected to be the highest percentage of the victims of this gender affirming hormone treatment, gender affirming surgery, genital mutilation surgeries and procedures and other efforts to convert the young and vulnerable among this population to this unhealthy and destructive lifestyle. In fact, I have heard reports indicating that the leading provider of abortion services are seeking to provide gender affirming hormone treatments and other transgender related treatments to members of this community.

14. To support and promote the same sex sexual practices of homosexual, lesbian, transgender, and other members of the LGBTQ+ communities, and their agenda is to support and promote perversion, harm, and to stymie the healthy growth and development of the members of this community, those who are proselytized by them, and others impacted by their propaganda, practices, and agenda.

Any individual or organization, including members of the religious community, who believe and teach that those who refuse to accept homosexuality are homophobic, and therefore harmful to this community, are not able to use the Bible or any Judeo-Christian principles or teachings to support their position. Many of these religious leaders, who once believed and taught that being homosexual was wrong, have changed their position and are now joining the affirmation crowd. They are now supporting this lifestyle and joining the voices of those who say anyone who does not support the homosexual lifestyle is homophobic, anti-Christian, and causes harm to this community. However, these people, "Christian leaders" and others, either do not use scriptures to support their position or use generic scriptures that they wrongly interpret and wrongly apply.

15. Many well-meaning people may think that passing laws and engaging in other efforts to affirm, promote the acceptance, practice, growth, and advancement of the sexual practices of homosexual, lesbians, transgenders, and other members of the LGBTQ+ communities are acts of love. However, they are as wrong as a person who is an enabler and provides drugs to a drug addict, alcohol to an alcoholic, or money to a person with a gambling addiction to support them and to show love toward them. "Love does no wrong to others, so love fulfills the requirements of God's law." (Romans 13:10, NLT).

16. Any medical provider or other person who provides gender-affirming hormones, performs body altering surgeries, deceitfully called "gender affirming" or sex reassignment surgeries on a child, or any other person, to amputate their breasts, their genitals, or any other part of their body, is in violation of the Hippocratic Oath to do no harm, and to abstain from all intentional wrongdoing, especially when these surgeries and treatments are performed on those in the puberty and adolescent stages of their lives. Minors are known to be naïve, impulsive, and are naturally going through a stage of life where they are suffering from identity crises. Many in the LGBTQ+ communities and others are attempting to take advantage of these young people at their most unstable and vulnerable stages of life.

17. Those who are providing or otherwise facilitating the provision of gender-affirming hormones and gender-affirming or sex reassignment surgeries are not willing to be held accountable for your, or anyone else's short- or long-term side effects of such treatment. You and your parent, your caretaker, or other person who love and cares for you will be on your own. Neither will the members of the LGBTQ+ communities that encouraged you to get such treatments be there for you for the long haul. The probability is nil.

18. Performing such sexual operations on children should be illegal and those who do so should be held accountable for the harm they cause. People are less likely to cause harm or engage in behavior that is likely to cause harm when they know they will be held accountable.

19. Very few, if any, who promote or perform gender affirming surgeries or hormone treatments on you, your child or anyone you love, and care about, can honestly say that they really care in the least about the long-term health and well-being of those on whom they perform such surgeries or provide such treatments.

If anyone who is either assisting in providing you with, or otherwise encouraging you to take gender affirming hormones, gender affirming surgeries or sex reassignment surgeries, tells you that they are doing it because they care about your health and well-being, ask them the following questions:

- What are the potential side effects of these treatments?

- Are there any longitudinal or other long-term studies of the outcomes of those who have had gender affirming surgeries and hormone treatment?

- What are the results? What percentage of those surveyed are yet suffering from mental illness or substance use disorder, post treatment?

- What percentage wish they had never gotten the treatment? What percentage continue to report having suicidal ideation?

- What percentage have attempted suicide post treatment?

- What percentage have committed suicide post treatment?

- What percentage report that their mental health symptoms didn't change after they got the treatment?

- What percentage report that their mental health condition got worse after the treatment?

- What percentage report they are having severe mental health issues for the first time, post treatment?

- Do they personally know of anyone who has had these treatments and has regretted it?

- Do they know of any actual side effects that those who have had these treatments have had?

- Based on my sexual and reproductive health and rights, do I have the right to choose whom I seek counseling and therapy from, including but not limited to, my pastor, Christian counselor, therapist, or other organization that does not offer or provide abortions or gender-affirming treatments?

- How long will the person who performs the surgeries or provides the hormone treatments be there for you after you receive these treatments?

- How often can you call them?

- Can you call them anytime, day or night, when you are suffering from the side effects of such treatment?

- Will they continue to support you and help you after you have gotten the treatment, outside of supplying you with medication?

- How long will you have to take medication for this treatment?

- What happens if you stop taking medication?

- Will they help you pay for any medical or mental health treatments that may result from this treatment if you need it?

- More importantly, ask them, should you change your mind about your identity and you realize that you made a mistake, ask whether you will be able to switch back to the way you were before you had the surgery or treatment?

- Will anyone be able to restore to you what you lost, or what was taken from you?

20. The agenda, same sex practices, and teachings of the members of the LGBTQ communities and those who promote and support such teaching are anti-Christ, anti-Christianity, and reject the teachings of scripture regarding this subject.

21. Females were made exclusively to be complementary to males biologically, emotionally, socially, and sexually.

22. Only biological females have the capability to completely complement the male.

23. Man, woman, mankind, humankind, male and female are not simply identities that are based on empirical evidence, social constructs, or sex arbitrarily assigned at birth, but are divine characterizations. Therefore, to deny or reject these characterizations is to reject the truth of God and call God a lie. Biological sex is not a personal decision, it's a scientific and divine reality.

24. No human sexual union of the same sex can cleave together in such a way to achieve the level of overall intimacy and fulfilment that can be achieved with the sexual union of a male and female, regardless as to how much they "love" each other due to their biopsychosocial and sexual makeup.

25. While I recognize and whole heartedly agree that every homosexual, lesbian, transgender person, and other member of the LGBTQ+ community should have the same constitutional rights as every other American, both as an American and as a human being, without regards to their sexuality, I further assert unequivocally that those rights include the right to marry whom they will in accordance with any law, be intimate and sexual with whom they will in accordance with the law and create intimate sexual partnerships with whom they will in according to the laws. However, I also recognize that according to the Judeo-Christian Bible and the laws and commandments of God, those sexual relationships are morally wrong, biblically wrong, and detestable in the sight of God and as such, as with each of us, those who engage in such behaviors will have to give account to God at the end of the day. "For we must all appear before the judgment seat of Christ, that each one may receive the things *done* in the body, according to what he has done, whether good or bad." (2 Corinthians 5:10, NKJV)

26. I also strongly disagree with the claims that the fight of the homosexual, lesbian, transgender, and other members of the LGBTQ+ community, which is a fight regarding the acceptance and advancement of their sexual interests, choices, desires, feelings, likes, dislikes, and preferences, are comparable to those of the civil rights struggles of the African American community of the fifties and sixties. Many African Americans were legally segregated, ostracized, discriminated against, humiliated, rejected, demeaned, alienated, physically, emotionally psychologically and sexually abused, falsely accused, wrongfully arrested, convicted, and imprisoned, dehumanized, terrorized, and murdered solely because of the color of their skin, an immutable characteristic. "...Can the Ethiopian change his skin, or the leopard his spots?" (Jeremiah 13:23, KJV) Therefore, for homosexual, lesbian, transgender, or other members of the LGBTQ+ communities to use the civil rights movement as a basis of their argument in support of their lifestyle is to simply hijack the civil rights movement. There is no moral equivalence.

27. Homosexual, lesbian, transgender, and other members of the LGBTQ+ sexual practices, affections, passions, and desires are biological and physical experiences that are driven by many factors, including but not limited to cultural, peer to peer, political, television media, social medial, social, psychological, emotional, legal, and spiritual influences.

28. God has never pronounced condemnation on an immutable characteristic, such as the color of a person's skin, as He does on homosexuality.

29. The root cause of homosexuality is spiritual and is the result of the rejection of the truths and revelations of God, which results in a reprobate mind and opens people up to the lies, deceptions, and access of Satan.

30. There is no scientific evidence to support homosexuality as an immutable characteristic.

31. There is empirical evidence that one can change from being a homosexual, lesbian, transgender and from other same sex interests and behaviors that include changing from having homosexual desires, passions and from the practice of homosexuality.

32. Because homosexual behavior is not physically compatible sexual behavior, it has a higher risk of infections, including AIDS, other sexually transmitted infections, and physical trauma as the homosexual attempt to sexualize parts of the body that were not made or meant for sexual activity. The truth is, just because a body part is richly supplied with nerve endings that doesn't also then mean that it is to be sexualized or is there for sexual purposes.

33. Rather than recognizing the dangers that are inherent in homosexual sex and the harmful effects thereof, members of the homosexual, lesbian, transgender, and LGBTQ+ communities seek for a prophylactic or otherwise to be more creative. A prophylactic may prevent some diseases, but there is no prophylactic to ultimately protect against the consequences of sin.

34. Homosexuality is socially harmful.

While homosexuality is unequivocally considered a sin by the Bible, being a sin is not the worst thing about homosexuality as other sins are just as harmful, and some are more harmful. A huge difference, and the thing that makes homosexuality, lesbianism, transgenderism and the agenda and practices of this community so harmful, is the "in your face", "down your throat" forced acceptance and affirmation of their beliefs, practices, agenda, and lifestyle on others. This forced acceptance and forced affirmation is obtained by lobbyists, politicians, governmental entities, legislatures, court decisions, public service agencies, departments of education, school boards, city councils, governmental mandates, schools, including every level from preschool through university, women's sports, peer pressure, misguided religious leaders and religious organizations. Most people are good and respectful of the right of others to live their lives as they please and recognize that they are accountable for their own choices. However, most people, including parents, do not want to be forced to change their values and beliefs, especially their religious beliefs, just to accommodate or affirm the sinful, corrupt, and perverted values of any person or group. One thing that has been proven to be true is that homosexuality is like a cancer, it just keeps on spreading. At first the community said they only wanted the right to be free to live their lives as they chose. That is no longer sufficient. Now, that is so far from what they want. Today they want to change scientific and biblical truths such as the definition of a woman or man, male or female and deny their realities. They want to sexualize minor children and take away the God-given rights of parents to both teach and provide counseling and direction to their own children regarding their bodies and sexual matters. They are not content to just live and let live, they want to force themselves, their sexual practices, and agenda on the whole of society irrespective of their beliefs and values.

35. Homosexuality is emotionally and mentally harmful.

According to a study by Centers for Disease Control and Prevention: Gay and Bisexual Men's Health, "Gay, bisexual, and other men who have sex with men are at even greater risk for suicide attempts, especially before the age of 25. A study of youth in grades 7-12 found that lesbian, gay, and bisexual youth were more than twice as likely to have attempted suicide as their heterosexual peers." Retrieved from https://www.cdc.gov/msmhealth/suicide-violence-prevention.htm.

According to a report by the Newport Academy, 70 percent of LGBTQ teens experienced Symptoms of anxiety in the past year. 57 percent of LGBTQ teens experienced symptoms of Depression. Among all LGBTQ youth surveyed (ages 13-24), 81 percent wanted mental healthcare in the past year. However, 56 percent of those youth were unable to access care."

Retrieved from "https://www.newportacademy.com/resources/mental-health/lgbt-suicide-rates/"

Many will claim that the causes of these disturbing statistics are due to the rejection and other negative treatment of homosexuals. I posit that these stats are significantly higher among the homosexual population because the same spirit that causes homosexual desires and interests, turns on the homosexual, or otherwise opens the homosexual up to other spirits such as suicide, emotional disturbances, depression, anxiety, and other mental health issues. These disturbing statistics will certainly increase so long as there are those who deny the mental health component and block efforts to provide mental health intervention to this population.

As mental health and substance use disorders are said to be bidirectional, so it may also be said that homosexuality may be bidirectional with mental illness and substance use disorders. Each one may be a contributing factor to trigger the other.

Therefore, to outlaw intervention is harmful and may rob the homosexual and the transgender person of the intervention they desperately need. As such, it may be difficult to tell, in many cases, which came first, homosexuality or mental illness.

36. Homosexuality is spiritually harmful.

Since homosexual, lesbian, and transgender practices are disobedience of the Word and the commandments of God, they interferes with a person's relationship with God and are therefore spiritually harmful. All sin has a negative impact on our fellowship with God.

"If you keep my commands, you will remain in my love, just as I have kept my father's commands and remain in his love. I have told you this so that my joy may be in you and that your joy may be complete." (John 15:10-11, NIV) (See 1 Corinthians 6:9, NLT, listed above)

"Run from sexual sin! No other sin so clearly affects the body as this one does. For sexual immorality is a sin against your own body. Don't you realize that your body is the temple of the Holy Spirit, who lives in you and was given to you by God? You do not belong to yourself, for God bought you with a high price. So you must honor God with your body." (1 Corinthians 6:18-20, NLT)

37. In addition to mental illness, there is also a high rate of substance use disorder among the homosexual, lesbian, transgender, and members of the LGBTQ+ community. As mental health and substance use disorders are said to be bidirectional, so it may also be said that homosexuality may be bidirectional with substance use disorders. That being the case, each one may be a contributing factor to trigger the other. Since substance use disorder and homosexuality are in some cases bidirectional, it may be difficult to tell, in these cases, which came first, homosexuality or substance use disorders. As it causes more harm than good to outlaw intervention for a homosexual who is suffering from mental illness, so it is also potentially harmful to deny treatment interventions to a homosexual who is suffering from substance use disorder. Denying treatment that addresses both the substance use disorder and homosexuality will arguably rob the homosexual, lesbian, transgender, and other members of the LGBTQ+ community of the therapeutic intervention they desperately need to recover. If a person is suffering from mental illness, substance use disorder, or other disorder of any kind, that person's illness or disorder should be addressed as are others who suffer from these conditions. The fact that a homosexual, lesbian, transgender, or LGBTQ+ person is suffering from these conditions is no reason to accept, promote or support or affirm the homosexual lifestyle. The person should be treated the same way heterosexuals are treated. It is not helpful to simply blame all the mental and emotional health issues of the homosexual on the people who disagree with them and refuse to affirm their lifestyle. It is generally not harmful to consult and be evaluated by a mental health professional who does not have an agenda and will provide an unbiased, objective mental health assessment.

38. There are no reasons to create a special category for members of the homosexual, lesbian, transgender, and LGBTQ+ communities, nor to treat them as if they are a special class of people solely based on their sexual orientation, desires, interests, or preferences.

Just as important, there should be no efforts to push their lifestyle choices down the throats of others, especially on minor children.

Homosexuals, lesbian, transgender, and other members of the LGBTQ+ community should simply be treated with respect, loving-kindness, tolerance, acceptance as a human being and a person, with equality, fairly and right in the manner every other human being is treated without regard to their sexual desires, sexual orientation, or sexual preferences.

39. To make it illegal to call a woman, whom God calls a woman, a woman, and to call a man, whom God calls a man, a man, and to require those who believe God to do so, is also requiring them to call God a lie regarding his characterization of the woman and the man. It is also to require them to violate their Judeo-Christian values and to utterly disregard and disrespect their religious conviction and freedoms. Christians also have a constitutional right to freedom of religion, freedom of speech, a right to be respected, treated with loving-kindness, tolerance, acceptance, as human beings and a person, a right to be treated with equality, fairly, and right in the same manner of the LGBTQ+ communities and every other American and every other human being is treated. No one should ever be required to go against their religious convictions simply to honor the fantasies of another.

40. As indicated in Genesis 6:19, male and female pairing is necessary for reproduction and for sustaining humanity, fowls of the air and the various living creatures of the land and of the sea.

"In a general sense reproduction is one of the most important concepts in biology: it means making a copy, a likeness, and thereby providing for the continued existence of species. Although reproduction is often considered solely in terms of the production of offspring in animals and plants, the more general meaning has far greater significance to living organisms. To appreciate this fact, the origin of life and the evolution of organisms must be considered. One of the first characteristics of life that emerged in primeval times must have been the ability of some primitive chemical system to make copies of itself."

While the author of this report appears to support evolution, this author categorically denies the theory of evolution. This author, to the contrary, categorically believes in the biblical report of creation by God regarding the world and all that therein is. "In the beginning God created the heaven and the earth." (Genesis 1:1, KJV) "So God created man in his own image, in the image of God created He him; male and female created He them. (Genesis 1:27, KJV) Therefore all replication and reproduction started subsequent to God's creation and consistent with God's creation.

THE BIBLE BASIS FOR A BIBLICAL WORLDVIEW OF SEX AS MALE AND FEMALE

GENESIS 1:26

"Then God said, 'Let us make mankind in our image, in our likeness, so that they may rule over the fish in the sea and the birds in the sky, over the livestock and all the wild animals, and over all the creatures that move along the ground.'" (NIV)

"Then God said, 'Let us make human beings in our image, to be like us. They will reign over the fish in the sea, the birds in the sky, the livestock, all the wild animals on the earth, and the small animals that scurry along the ground.'" (NLT)

"And God said, Let us make man in our image, after our likeness: and let them have dominion over the fish of the sea, and over the fowl of the air, and over the cattle, and over all the earth, and over every creeping thing that creepeth upon the earth." (KJV)

GENESIS 1:27

"So God created mankind in his own image, in the image of God he created them; male and female he created them." (NIV)

"So God created human beings in his own image. In the image of God he created them; male and female he created them." (NLT)

"So God created man in his *own* image, in the image of God created he him; male and female created he them." (KJV)

GENESIS 5:2

"He created them male and female and blessed them. And he named them 'Mankind' when they were created." (NIV)

"He created them male and female, and he blessed them and called them 'human.'" (NLT)

"Male and female created he them; and blessed them, and called their name Adam, in the day when they were created." (KJV)

GENESIS 6:19

"You are to bring into the ark two of all living creatures, male and female, to keep them alive with you." (NIV)

"Bring a pair of every kind of animal—a male and a female—into the boat with you to keep them alive during the flood." (NLT)

"And of every living thing of all flesh, two of every *sort* shalt thou bring into the ark, to keep *them* alive with thee; they shall be male and female." (KJV)

GENESIS 7:2

"Take with you seven pairs of every kind of clean animal, a male and its mate, and one pair of every kind of unclean animal, a male and its mate," (NIV)

"Take with you seven pairs—male and female—of each animal I have approved for eating and for sacrifice, and take one pair of each of the others." (NLT)

"Of every clean beast thou shalt take to thee by sevens, the male and his female: and of beasts that *are* not clean by two, the male and his female." (KJV)

GENESIS 7:3

"and also seven pairs of every kind of bird, male and female, to keep their various kinds alive throughout the earth." (NIV)

"Also take seven pairs of every kind of bird. There must be a male and a female in each pair to ensure that all life will survive on the earth after the flood." (NLT)

"Of fowls also of the air by sevens, the male and the female; to keep seed alive upon the face of all the earth." (KJV)

GENESIS 7:9

"male and female, came to Noah and entered the ark, as God had commanded Noah." (NIV)

"They entered the boat in pairs, male and female, just as God had commanded Noah." (NLT)

"There went in two and two unto Noah into the ark, the male and the female, as God had commanded Noah." KJV)

GENESIS 7:16

"The animals going in were male and female of every living thing, as God had commanded Noah. Then the LORD shut him in." (NIV)

"A male and female of each kind entered, just as God had commanded Noah. Then the LORD closed the door behind them." (NLT)

"And they that went in, went in male and female of all flesh, as God had commanded him: and the LORD shut him in." (KJV)

MATTHEW 19:4

"'Haven't you read,' he replied, 'that at the beginning the Creator 'made them male and female.'" (NIV)

"'Haven't you read the Scriptures?' Jesus replied. 'They record that from the beginning 'God made them male and female.'" (NLT)

"And he answered and said unto them, Have ye not read, that he which made *them* at the beginning made them male and female." (KJV)

MARK 10:6

"But at the beginning of creation God 'made them male and female.'" (NIV)

"But 'God made them male and female' from the beginning of creation.'" (NLT)

"But from the beginning of the creation God made them male and female." (KJV)

Right and wrong is determined by God, who is the creator of the universe and all that herein is. Wrong is identified as transgression, trespass, disobedience, and rebellion against the laws and commandments of God. Another term for disobeying God's Word and commandment is sin, which means to miss the mark.

According to 1 John 3:4 (KJV), "Whosoever committeth sin transgresseth also the law: for sin is the transgression of the law." The reference to law is a reference to God's law which is recorded in the Judeo-Christian bible.

Wrong is also indicated as a violation of one's nature. God has created man in such a way that, apart from any written law or moral codes, men have an innate and natural sense of sense of right and wrong written in their nature and in their hearts that informs them of what's right and wrong.

However, should one, for whatever the reason, feel in their nature that something is right or wrong, when they receive the law or any moral code of God, they will be held accountable to that law or code.

For example, according to Paul in Romans 2:14-15, men may rely on their nature when they don't have the actual written laws or Word of God.

"Indeed, when Gentiles, who do not have the law, do by nature things required by the law, they are a law for themselves, even though they do not have the law." (Romans 2:14, NIV) "Even Gentiles, who do not have God's written law, show that they know his law when they instinctively obey it, even without having heard it." (Romans 2:14, NLT)

"For when the Gentiles, which have not the law, do by nature the things contained in the law, these, having not the law, are a law unto themselves:" (Romans 2:14, KJV)

"They show that the requirements of the law are written on their hearts, their consciences also bearing witness, and their thoughts sometimes accusing them and at other times even defending them." (Romans 2:15, NIV)

"They demonstrate that God's law is written in their hearts, for their own conscience and thoughts either accuse them or tell them they are doing right." (Romans 2:15, NLT)

"Which shew the work of the law written in their hearts, their conscience also bearing witness, and *their* thoughts the mean while accusing or else excusing one another." (Romans 2:15, KJV)

Ultimately, things are not wrong based on cultural norms, legal precedence, Supreme Court rulings, governmental decrees, or other mandates by man. Things are ultimately right or wrong based on what God has determined to be right or wrong and what He has written into man's nature. For instance, it is natural for a male to be sexually attracted to a female. It's written into his nature. When it's the opposite, it's unnatural and against nature, and consequently against the plan and created work of God. Things can be right according to the laws, decrees, and rulings of man and wrong in the sight of God. Every behavior, sexual or otherwise, that God prohibits is wrong and is a sin.

CONCLUSION

When human beings are viewed sexually, there are two sexes. These two sexes are defined as male and female. From a biblical perspective, when human beings are considered sexually, they are defined as such solely based on their physical and biological makeup. Both males and females have distinct physical, biological, and sexual characteristics which are determinate as to whether they are male or female. In fact, it is these distinct characteristics that determines their sex and whether a person is a male or a female.

HOPE FOR HOMOSEXUALS AND MEMBERS OF THE LGBTQ COMMUNITY

Homosexuals are not another race of people, or another specimen of a human being, nor are they any different than any other human being. They are members of the human race and thus the same as every other human being. The only thing unique about homosexuals is their sexuality and all the related issues. Thus, when the scripture states, "For this is how God loved the world: He gave his one and only Son, so that everyone who believes in him will not perish but have eternal life." (John 3:16, NLT) and "For God did not send his son into the world to condemn the world, but to save the world through him." (John 3:17, NIV), that includes the homosexual. God does not discriminate against people as the scripture states, "Then Peter replied, 'I see very clearly that God shows no favoritism.'" (Acts 10:34, NLT).

Any human being who has not placed faith in Jesus as their Savior is not saved. That would include homosexuals, transgender persons, and every member of the LGBTQ communities. A person who is a homosexual can be saved as can every other human being who places faith in Jesus Christ as Savior. Thus a homosexual can change from being a homosexual in the same way an alcoholic can change from being alcoholic, a thief can change from being a thief, a prostitute can change from being a prostitute, a liar can change from being a liar, a gambler can change from being a gambler, a drug addict can change from being an addict, an adulterer can change from being an adulterer, and a person addicted to pornography can change from that addiction.

Salvation includes deliverance from the power of sin and Satan, deliverance from the ultimate punishment of sin, which is eternal separation from God. It also includes to heal, to make whole, to set free, to preserve, and to keep.

While I recognize that there are several effective interventions that have proven to be highly successful in helping people to effectively address various addictive and destructive behaviors and habits and obtain permanent deliverance from such behaviors, laws have been passed against using intervention to help the homosexual change.

Yet there is hope for the homosexual, transgender, and other members of the LGBTQ communities as change can come by hearing and believing the gospel of Jesus Christ and calling on the name of the Lord.

"And that message is the very message about faith that we preach: If you openly declare that Jesus is Lord and believe in your heart that God raised him from the dead, you will be saved. For it is by believing in your heart that you are made right with God, and it is by openly declaring your faith that you are saved. As the Scriptures tell us, "Anyone who trusts in him will never be disgraced "(Romans 10:9-11, NLT).

For "Everyone who calls on the name of the LORD will be saved." (Romans 10:17, NLT).

While anyone who places faith in Jesus will be immediately placed in a right standing with God, your life can also be changed because of this newfound faith.

WHAT DOES A CHANGED LIFE LOOK LIKE?

As noted above, the homosexual, transgender, and other members of the LGBTQ communities' lives are characterized by and replete with terms such as "Strong, persistent, and intense desire, strong preference, repeatedly stated desire, insistence, fantasies, marked incongruence, make believe, strong rejection and strong dislike." Every one of these terms are associated with our spirit and emotions and are realized in our passions, affections, and desires. They are all also dynamic and subjective. The salvation experience is specifically designed to deal with these experiences. Paul wrote to the church at Corinth where members of that church had been homosexuals among having other sinful and ungodly habits and behaviors. Paul wrote, "Don't you realize that those who do wrong will not inherit the Kingdom of God? Don't fool yourselves. Those who indulge in sexual sin, or who worship idols, or commit adultery, or are male prostitutes, or practice homosexuality, or are thieves, or greedy people, or drunkards, or are abusive, or cheat people—none of these will inherit the Kingdom of God. (1 Corinthians 6:9-10, NLT)

Jesus tells us that, "For out of the heart come evil thoughts: murder, adultery, sexual immorality, theft, false testimony, slander. These are what defile a person..." (Matthew 15:19a, NIV). The word defile means to desecrate, pollute, or otherwise make unclean.

Then Paul adds, "Some of you were once like that. But you were cleansed; you were made holy; you were made right with God by calling on the name of the Lord Jesus Christ and by the Spirit of our God." (1 Corinthians 6:11, NLT). Here, Paul categorically informs us that those who had been homosexuals were no longer homosexuals because they had been cleansed of this behavior, set apart from this behavior, set apart to God and made right with God.

Paul also, in his letter to the church at Galatia, told them,

"Those who belong to Christ Jesus have nailed the passions and desires of their sinful nature to his cross and crucified them there." (Galatians 5:24, NLT)

Paul also writes to Titus and asks him to remind those under his leadership, "Once, we, too, were foolish and disobedient. We were misled and became slaves to many lusts and pleasures. Our lives were full of evil and envy, and we hated each other. But when God our Savior revealed his kindness and love, he saved us, not because of the righteous things we had done, but because of is mercy. He washed away our sins, giving us a new birth and new life through the Holy Spirit. He generously poured out the Spirit upon us through Jesus Christ our Savior. Because of his grace he made us right in his sight and gave us confidence that we will inherit eternal life." (Titus 3:3-7, NLT).

"The Lord isn't really being slow about his promise, as some people think. No, he is being patient for your sake. He does not want anyone to be destroyed, but wants everyone to repent. (2 Peter 3:9, NLT). Jesus wants everyone to turn from their sins, to turn to faith in Jesus Christ for salvation and does not want anyone to be lost and eternally separated from Him.

FINALLY, THERE ARE A FEW BASIC STEPS TO BE SAVED

1. Acknowledge that you are a sinner and in need of a Savior.

   "If we claim we have no sin, we are only fooling ourselves and not living in the truth. But if we confess our sins to him, he is faithful and just to forgive us our sins and to cleanse us from all wickedness. If we claim we have not sinned, we are calling God a liar and showing that his word has no place in our hearts." (1 John 1:8-10, NLT)

2. Recognize that Jesus is that Savior.

   "Furthermore, we have seen with our own eyes and now testify that the Father sent his Son to be the Savior of the world." (1 John 4:14, NLT)

   "There is salvation in no one else! God has given no other name under heaven by which we must be saved." (Acts 4:12, NLT)

3. Place your faith in Jesus.

   "If you openly declare that Jesus is Lord and believe in your heart that God raised him from the dead, you will be saved. For it is by believing in your heart that you are made right with God, and it is by openly declaring your faith that you are saved." (Romans 10:9-10, NLT).

4. Ask him to fill you with His Spirit

   "Don't be drunk with wine, because that will ruin your life. Instead, be filled with the Holy Spirit..." (Ephesians 5:18, NLT).

   "And God has given us his Spirit as proof that we live in him and he in us." (1 John 4:13, NLT)

   "So, if you sinful people know how to give good gifts to your children, how much more will your heavenly Father give the Holy Spirit to those who ask him." (Luke 11:13, NLT).

5. If you don't have a church home, find a Bible-teaching church and join it for further instructions regarding how you should then live your life and what God expects of you as a believer in Jesus Christ.

"And let us not neglect our meeting together, as some people do, but encourage one another, especially now that the day of his return is drawing near. (Hebrews 10:25, NLT).

A SUGGESTED PRAYER
FOR SALVATION

Dear Jesus, I recognize that I am a sinner and in need of a Savior. Jesus, I also recognize You as that Savior. Forgive my sins and save me from my sins. I openly declare that Jesus is Lord and I believe in my heart that God raised Him from the dead. You said if I did this, I would be saved. You also said it is my believing in my heart what the Bible says about Jesus that will cause me to be made right with God, and it is my open declaration of my faith in Jesus that would cause me to be saved. Lord, I confess Jesus as Lord and believe in my heart. Thank You for saving me. Deliver me from everything that is contrary to Your will. Set me free and help me to live my life according to Your will in every area of life. Set me free from homosexuality, transgenderism, and the LGBTQ lifestyle and all ungodliness and unrighteousness, in Jesus' name, amen.

LISTING OF ALL REFERENCES FOR THE QUOTES USED IN THIS BOOK

American Psychiatric Association (1968) Diagnostic and Statistical Manual of Mental Disorders, (2nd ed). Retrieved from https://www.madinamerica.com/wp-content/uploads/2015/08/DSM-II.pdf

American Psychiatric Association (2000) *Diagnostic and Statistical Manual of Mental Disorders* (4th ed., text rev.) America Psychiatric Association, Washington D.C.

American Psychiatric Association (2013) *Diagnostic and Statistical Manual of Mental Disorders* (5th ed.) America Psychiatric Association, Washington D.C.

American Psychiatric Association (2022) *Diagnostic and Statistical Manual of Mental Disorders* (5th ed., text rev) America Psychiatric Association, Washington D.C.

Entwistle, D.N. (2010). *Integrative Approaches To Psychology nd Christianity: An Introduction Worldview Issues, Philosophical Foundations, And Models of Integration.* (2 ed.). Cascade Books

Goldenberg, H. & Goldenberg, I. (2013). *Family Therapy: An Overview.* (8th ed.). Brooks/Cole

Henley, T.B. (2019). *Hergenhahn's An Introduction to the History of Psychology.* (8th ed.). Cengage

AZQUOTES https://www.azquotes.com/quote/766608

A Hindu proverb states, "Denying the truth doesn't change the facts." (Author Unknown)

Arthur Schopenhauer. (n.d.). AZQuotes.com. Retrieved

November 13, 2023, from AZQuotes.com Web site: https://www.azquotes.com/quote/261903

ThoughtCo. 30 Quotes by Aristotle on Virtue, Government, Death and More Aristotle on Truth Retrieved from https://www.thoughtco.com/aristotle-quotes-117130

Medical Author: William C. Shiel Jr., MD, FACP, FACR

Definition of prophylactic retrieved from https://www.rxlist.com/prophylactic/definition.htm

Goodreads retrieved from https://www.goodreads.com/author/show/130074.Ryan_Bigge

Aldous Huxley – Perception Deception

Visweswaran Balasubramanian, What is Truth? A Philosophical Approach

Retrieved from https://timesofindia.indiatimes.com/readers-blog/mycosmos/what-is-truth-a-philosophical-approach-28803/. https://www.relicsworld.com/aristotle/

RelicsWorld_A World of Words Which Can Change Your Life: Aristotle Quotes Right to Life Michigan Retrieved from (https://rtl.org/multicultural-outreach/black-abortion-statistics/).

Aristotle quote retrieved from https://www.azquotes.com/quote/766608

Retrieved from https://www.goodreads.com/author/show/130074.Ryan_Bigge

Edward de Bono, "Perception is real even when it is not reality." Retrieved from https://www.azquotes.com/author/1649-Edward_de_Bono/tag/perception

Retrieved from https://www.spiked-online.com/2023/02/05/dr-john-money-and-the-sinister-origins-of-gender-ideology/.

Retrieved from https://www.coe.int/en/web/gender-matters/sex-and-gender#:

Retrieved from https://www.google.com/search?q=instinct+meaning

Retrieved from (https://rtl.org/multicultural-outreach/black-abortion-statistics/).

Retrieved from (https://www.cdc.gov/msmhealth/suicide-violence-prevention.htm).

Retrieved from https://www.newportacademy.com/resources/mental-health/lgbt-suicide-rates/"

Retrieved from https://www.britannica.com/science/reproduction-biology

SCRIPTURE INDEX

8:44
10:10
14:6
15:10-11
16:12-14
17:17
18:38

Acts
4:12
10:34

Romans
1:18-28
2:14-15
10:9-11
10:17
11:33
13:10
14:17

1 Corinthians
4:20
6:9-11
6:12-14
6:15-20
7:32-35
11:8-9
11:11-12

2 Corinthians
5:10
13:8

Galatians
4:16
5:19
5:24

Ephesians
5:18
5:28-29a
5:31

2 Thessalonians
2:11

1 Timothy
1:8-10

2 Timothy
1:10
2:7

Titus
1:2
3:3-7

Hebrews
1:7
6:18
10:25

James
2:26
3:14

2 Peter
2:2
3:9

1 John
1:8-10
2:21
3:4
4:13-14

Jude
1:7

Revelations
2:14

REFERRALS

Focus On the Family
Phone: 1-800-A-Family (232-6459)
Help@FocusontheFamily.com
https://www.focusonthefamily.com/

PROlife Across AMERICA
Phone: 800-366-7773
https://prolifeacrossamerica.org/

National Right to Life
National Office – Mailing Address
PO Box 96498
Washington, DC 20077-7606
Phone: 202-626-8820
https://www.nrlc.org/

Catholic Charities USA
2050 Ballenger Ave,
Suite 400
Alexandria, VA 22314
Phone: 703-549-1390
https://www.catholiccharitiesusa.org

Tim Tebow Foundation
https://timtebowfoundation.org/
7700 Square Lake Blvd.
Jacksonville, FL 32256
Phone: 904-380-8499

Disclaimer: The above referrals are made arbitrarily by the author for the sake of those who may need these services. The referrals do not claim or is in any way intended to indicate that any of the organizations listed above agree with, have a relationship with, or are connected to the author or otherwise support any of the statements or opinions of the author listed herein. Anyone who chooses to utilize these services are advised to do their own due diligence regarding the use of any of the referral services listed above, as with all service providers, in order to be able to make an informed decision as to whether the services offered by these providers are right for them.

Milton Keynes UK
Ingram Content Group UK Ltd.
UKHW050634150424
441175UK00013B/461